GETTING INTO L

For many years I was content with a robotic commitment to my religion. That is, I was reading, repeating words or phrases, but without a complete understanding of the scripture nor a complete <u>feeling</u> of the emotional depth for Jesus. Subsequent to our eye and heart-opening trip to Israel several years ago, I no longer wanted to be a "robot". I needed, and deeply desired, a closer *relationship* with GOD. My wife, Sandra, encouraged me to read, study, and <u>live</u> the Christian Bible for which I am forever grateful. The Bible has created an insatiable thirst in me for GOD's "Word" and the life-giving teachings of Jesus. It has given me the comfort, peace, and confidence to address all the trials and tribulations of this world, as well as the euphoric realization of GOD's promise of His priceless gift of eternal life. It is, by far, the most amazing book I have ever read.

The apostle Peter told us: "Like newborn babies, you must crave pure spiritual milk so that you will grow into a full experience of salvation. Cry out for this nourishment, now that you have had a taste of the Lord's kindness." 1 Peter 2:2-3. Have you ever made the following comment, or something similar? "Wow, if I would have known that, I would have done this years ago!" The "wow" is the Bible -- and Jesus is anxiously awaiting your arrival.

The following observations, experiences, comments, stories, are all reflected against my reading of the Bible. They are all designed to give you "something to think about" during your individual journey with the LORD. I do not intend my "writings" to be an in-depth treatise on the Christian Bible, nor do I seek any literary recognition. My sole purpose is to connect the reader by some recognized words, happenings, quotes, stories, experiences, or observations that might generate a genuine and realistic <u>spiritual meaning</u> which, in turn, will lead to an acceptance of Jesus Christ into one's life. "And you must show mercy to those whose faith is wavering. *<u>Rescue others by snatching them from the flames of judgment.</u>*" Jude 22-23

By no means do I intend any judgment, criticism, or disrespect of anyone who has a different viewpoint.

You can read the "writings" at your own pace. But my hope is that you will concentrate and ruminate on the Scripture and thoughts in each for perhaps *a week* before moving to the next one. Reading more than one at a time could result in not focusing on the individual message GOD intends for you from each writing. I am hopeful that you will read the essay more than once (perhaps every day or every other day), digest it; let it "live" with you throughout the week.

I encourage you to have your Bible with you when you read so you can look up the references and read along. It will help you understand the meaning and depth of the writing. Additionally, you will familiarize yourself with the Bible, and be encouraged to future reading, for a more content, joy-filled life.

JUSUS IS YOUR MOTIVATION AND YOUR DESTINATION.

WHAT'S INSIDE.

1. THREE TO GET READY
2. GOD'S VIEW VS MAN'S VIEW OF THE WORLD
3. FORGIVES AND FORGETS
4. DAILY PRAISE AND THANKSGIVING
5. WHY WAS I BORN?
6. BAGGAGE, PLEASE
7. ACCEPTANCE
8. LOTTO
9. WINNING TEAM
10. IF NOT JESUS, WHO?
11. ABORTION
12. ABORTION AFTERMATH
13. REDEEMER REMINDER
14. SURVIVOR OR CASUALTY
15. SURVIVOR OR CASUALTY (WEEK TWO)
16. THREE STRIKES AND YOU'RE OUT!
17. SALVATION DEADLINE
18. ACE IN THE HOLE
19. FORGIVENESS: THE TOUGHEST TEST OF LOVE
20. LAST CHANCE CONVERSATION
21. LIVING EQUALITY
22. FAILURE TO COMMUNICATE
23. THE DEVIL MADE ME DO IT
24. I AM THE GREATEST
25. EINSTEIN FOR JESUS

26. THE CONDITION OF YOUR CONDITION

27. LOST AND FOUND

28. UNFATHOMABLE

29. DON'T PUT THE CART BEFORE THE HORSE

30. QUIT COMPLAINING AND DO WHAT I SAY!

31. I WANT THE TRUTH. YOU CAN'T HANDLE THE TRUTH!

32. REFUSING THE WORD AND JESUS

33. SHIP OF FOOLS

34. DON'T MISS THE OPPORTUNITY TO STRIKE WHILE THE IRON IS HOT

35. DEAD INSIDE

36. THE BULLPEN

37. EXPERT ADVICE AND ASSISTANCE

38. LOVE CONQUERS ALL

39. BODY OR SOUL

40. KISS

41. GOD'S SILVER LINING

42. LIVE OR DIE

43. THE HAPPINESS OF FORGIVENESS

44. PEER PRESSURE

45. IF I WERE A RICH MAN.....

46. GOD'S VIEW, TWO WORDS, AND ONE MAN

47. PERSONALIZING LIFE'S JOURNEY (TAKE IT PERSONALLY)

48. RECOGNIZING GOD'S HINTS

49. THE LITTLE ENGINE THAT COULD

50. SCARED THE DEVIL OUT OF ME

51. STOP, LOOK AND LISTEN
52. THIS IS FOR ALL THE MARBLES
53. I WANT YOUR WILL TO BE DONE, NOT MINE
54. HELP NEEDED, OR JUST PLAIN LAZY
55. NEVER GIVE UP
56. JUDGEMENT
57. NEVER RELINQUISH THE PROGRESS MADE
58. SEARCHING FOR THE TRUTH
59. A MOMENT OF RIGHTEOUSNESS
60. ABSORBING THE DEATH AND THE RESURRECTION OF JESUS
61. THE DIRECTNESS OF JESUS
62. SOUL WINNER.
63. ALL FOR ONE AND ONE FOR ALL
64. GOD'S SPIRITUAL HOME RUN WITH FRANCIS OF ASSISI
65. WAR WITH HELL
66. JESUS, THE GREATEST WITNESS EVER
67. MEDIATOR
68. SPIRITUAL WISDOM
69. KNOWING GOD'S WILL FOR YOU
70. BOOMERANG
71. OUR FATHER WHO ART IN HEAVEN
72. THE LITTLE RED HEN
73. NO WAY, ABSOLUTELY NO WAY
SOME OF GOD'S POSITIVES (POINTS FOR REFERENCE)
ABOUT THE AUTHOR

ACKNOWLEDGEMENTS.

My most sincere and deep personal thanks to Derik
Hines, good friend, gifted pastor and teacher at Life
Church, Peoria, Arizona and to Brian Glubish, Canadian
New Testament professor and good friend. Also, I thank
my friends in small group Bible study, plus many others
who help me learn, encourage my walk, and urge me to
write.

And the biggest thanks to my wife, Sandra. She is my
encouragement, my support, my friend, my companion,
my partner, and my love. Additionally, she, with her
journalism background, spent many hours editing my
grammar for clarity sake, engaging considered discussion,
and making constructive suggestions without changing
my intended message. She made my writings more
concise and palatable. She is and will always be "my
lady".

I would be totally remiss if I failed to thank and praise the
Lord, God Almighty. "What do you have that God hasn't
given you? And if everything you have is from God, why
boast as though it were not a gift?"   1 Corinthians 4:7.

"For the wisdom of this world is foolishness to God."

1 *Corinthians 3:19*

Something to think about.

1. THREE TO GET READY.

Before we start our journey, I believe to fully build understanding of the weekly devotional meditations, you need to read and digest the *foundation* of my premises via the following three principles:

1. GOD's View vs Man's View of The World.

2. GOD Forgives and Forgets.

3. Daily Praise and Thanksgiving to GOD.

I've developed the above principles individually in the next three meditations of your book.

Additionally, in the back of this booklet is *"Some of GOD's Positives"*. Life seems so full of negatives. So, I have listed *some* of the positives GOD has promised in His Word that we can choose to receive from HIM on a daily basis. Review these now and often. Feel the love and GOD's desire for a personal relationship with you. AND, know that under <u>no circumstances</u> will GOD abandon you.

Something to think about.

1

2. GOD'S VIEW VS. MAN'S VIEW OF THE WORLD.

Begin with this *absolute.* There is a difference between how GOD views the world and how man views the world; between GOD's hands and the hands of man; between earthly ways and spiritual ways. We have been put on notice: "*My thoughts are not your thoughts, neither are your ways my ways*", declares the Lord. Isaiah 55:8. "The Lord does not look at the things man looks at. Man looks at the <u>outward appearance</u>, but the Lord <u>looks at the heart.</u>" 1 Samuel 16:7.

Man's view: Outward appearance---a good physique, handsome, tall, other physical qualities, status, wealth, achievements, and possessions, all of which show a love for the things of this world. When man loves this world, he follows the desires of his sinful nature, the results are sexual immorality, lustful pleasures, idolatry, hostility, quarreling, jealousy, outbursts of anger, selfish ambition, envy, greed, drunkenness, wild parties, and other like sins. Anyone living that sort of life will not inherit the Kingdom of GOD. (see Galatians 5:19-21). This world, and all its cravings, is under the control of the devil (see 1 John 5:19).

GOD's view: Jesus! GOD chose you to be the holy people He loves, so clothe yourself with tenderhearted mercy, kindness, humility, gentleness, patience and above all, love; forgive anyone who offends you; <u>and let the peace that comes from Christ Jesus rule in your hearts</u> (see Colossians 3:12-15). Jesus leads you to the Father and to His Kingdom.

You have to live *with* man, but you don't have to *think* like him! The apostle Paul told us how to transition out of thinking like a man. "Don't copy the behavior and customs of this world, <u>but let God transform you into a new person by CHANGING THE WAY YOU THINK. Then you will learn to know God's will for you, which is good and pleasing and perfect.</u>" Romans 12:2. With God's help, you can change your thinking so it coincides with how God views the world.

God views your "heart- produced" conduct for your judgment. He can easily determine if you lived man's view with the devil or God's view with Jesus. If it is the devil you will leave this life with Satan--forever; if it is Jesus, you will leave this life with Jesus--forever. No <u>loopholes</u> with God.

Something to think about.

3. FORGIVES AND FORGETS.

Let's continue our journey with Hebrews 8:12 because it is a promise from GOD you should always remember. It is so very powerful; one you will recall each time you visit with GOD about the salvation of your soul. It provides for complete trust in GOD, comfort to us as sinners, forgiveness beyond comprehension, speechless humility, proof of GOD's *unconditional* love and mercy, plus guidance in dealings with our fellow man.

"And I will forgive their wickedness, and *I will never again remember their sins.*" Hebrews 8:12. Yes! GOD forgives *and* forgets.

Each evening, during your day's end visit with GOD. You can confess and truly repent for the sins of the day as well as any past sins, and wake up with a clean slate. *Whatever* sins you have committed in the past are forgiven, forgotten, and will not be used to prevent entry into heaven on your judgment day. This is GOD's promise.

From the book, *"The Ragamuffin Gospel"*, authored by Brennan Manning, is the following story. There was rumor that a Catholic woman had visions of Jesus. Heard by an archbishop, he inquired of the woman if the rumor was true. The woman assured him it was fact. The archbishop requested that when the woman next spoke with Jesus would she ask Jesus what the archbishop's sins were at his last confession. Woman: "Did I hear you right, Bishop? You actually want me to ask Jesus to tell me the sins of your past?" The bishop said, "exactly" and asked her to let him know if anything happens. Ten days later the woman notified the bishop of her recent apparition. She told the bishop that she had asked Jesus to tell her the sins that the bishop had last confessed.

Bishop: "What did Jesus say?"

Woman: "Bishop, -- these are his exact words: I CAN'T REMEMBER!!!"

Clean slate each new day. GOD DOES NOT LIE!

REMEMBER this, and daily go to Him for His promised forgiveness.

Something to think about.

* (published by Multnomah Books, Colorado Springs, Colorado, Copyright 1990.)

4. DAILY PRAISE AND THANKSGIVING.

Having digested promises in the past two essays, "GOD's View of the World" and GOD "Forgives and Forgets", there is one additional principle of acceptance and understanding I hope you'll add to the foundation as you launch into considering the remaining essays before you. That principle is that it is our obligation to DAILY praise and thank GOD for all He has done. GOD created the world for our enjoyment and created us for the sole purpose of enjoying salvation with Him. <u>EVERYTHING we have comes from GOD.</u>

"You do not belong to yourself, for GOD bought you with a high price." (meaning Jesus) 1 Corinthians 6:19-20. "I plead with you to give your bodies to God <u>because of all He has done for you.</u> Let them be a living and holy sacrifice -- the kind he will find acceptable. This is truly the way to worship Him." Romans 12:1.

Jesus said: "You must love the LORD your GOD with all your heart, all your soul, and all your mind." Matthew 22:37.

In today's busy world, you might have multiple interests, employment duties, parental obligations, military responsibilities, retirement commitments, sports activities, enjoyment of the world GOD created, and many others. This is all well and good, but <u>each day</u>, remember

-- NOTHING is more important than praising and thanking GOD for all He has done, and does.

John, one of the gospel writers, made this abundantly clear: "Dear children, <u>keep away from anything that might take GOD's place in your hearts.</u>" 1 John 5:21.

Even with all our obligations, it is a must!

"You must have the same attitude that Jesus had."

Philippians 2:5

5. WHY WAS I BORN?

Mark Twain once said: "The two most important days in your life are the day you were born and the day you find out why!" If true, then we must find out the "why day" as soon as possible. During my lifetime I have observed people wandering about seeking a perceived philosophical answer or becoming caught up in some mental resolution exercise to "find themselves". Confucius said: "Life is really simple, but we insist on making it complicated."

GOD has already simplified our lives with His <u>plan</u> for each of us: "Even before He made the world, GOD loved us and chose us in Christ to be holy and without fault in His eyes. GOD decided in advance to adopt us into His own family by bringing us to Himself through Jesus Christ. This is what he wanted to do, and it gave Him great pleasure. So, we praise GOD for the glorious grace He has poured out on us who belong to his dear Son. He is so rich in kindness and grace that He purchased our freedom with the <u>blood of his Son</u> and forgave our sins". Ephesians 1:4-7.

<u>GOD didn't create us to watch us die, HE CREATED US TO WATCH US *LIVE*---- WITH HIM ---- FOREVER!</u>

Something to think about.

6. BAGGAGE, PLEASE.

"Baggage" has been described as a psychological burden that feels like a curse. Often, guilt and regret keep us stuck in thinking about the past. "You cannot change your beginning, but you can start where you are and change the ending." (C.S. Lewis).

Think of your baggage. Now let's review some real baggage, as per a few recognized heroes of the Bible, all of whom went on to love and effectively serve the LORD. They were forgiven, forgot the past, and focused on the future.

Moses: observed an Egyptian soldier beating a slave. Moses killed the soldier and buried him in the sand. (murder).

David: had an adulterous affair with Bathsheba; then made sure her husband was killed in battle; later marrying Bathsheba. (adultery, murder, covet neighbor's wife).

Peter: traveled with Jesus for years, yet denied knowing Jesus three times after Jesus was arrested -- before the cock crowed. (unbeliever, coward, liar).

Paul: before he became perhaps the greatest disciple of Jesus Christ, Paul spent years killing Christians. (multiple murders---he was judge and jury).

Your "baggage" is undoubtedly pale when compared to the above individuals. Jesus asks you to give Him your weariness and heavy burdens, and He will find rest for your soul (see Matthew 11:28-29). GIVE YOUR BAGGAGE TO JESUS!

"And I will forgive their wickedness, and I will never again remember their sins." (Hebrews 8:12). If GOD forgives and forgets, why are YOU remembering?

Baggage gone-----baggage forgotten! Focus on what lies ahead -- salvation.

Something to think about.

7. ACCEPTANCE.

FACTS: You are traveling in rural Wyoming in February and your motor vehicle stalls. It is 20 degrees below zero; nighttime; wind blowing; no one else on the highway. You are alone. Fortunately, you do have a cell phone and there is service. Your call is successful, and the garage will send someone out as quickly as they can. It has been 45 minutes; you are anxious, cold, and prayerful. There is no question that when the repair truck arrives the person inside can fix your auto; warmth will be restored, and you can get on your way. The repair truck arrives!

Question: Would you care if the person stepping out of the repair truck is male or female, republican or democrat, conservative or liberal, very tall or a midget, carries a gun, multiple tattoos, fat or skinny, a recent parolee? How about race, creed, or color? Is there any reason whatsoever that would make this person an unacceptable helper?

Man's view of acceptance: often our acceptance is based on what others think--- we want to "fit in", garner approval. And at times we might have difficulty tolerating the differences and diversity outlined in the question above.

God's view of acceptance: UNCONDITIONAL. God doesn't care about "outward appearances", "labels", or "categories". "There is no longer Jew or Gentile, slave or free, male and female. <u>For you are all one in Christ Jesus.</u>" Galatians 3:28. "Love each other in the same way I have loved you." John 15:12.

<u>GOD ACCEPTS YOU THE WAY YOU ARE.</u> <u>ARE YOU PREPARED TO LOVE AND ACCEPT OTHERS THE WAY THEY ARE?</u>

Something to think about.

8. LOTTO.

Facts: You are on leave from the United States Army and while at home you discover in your jean jacket a lotto ticket. You recall that before you entered the service you attended a Twins baseball game in Minneapolis and bought the ticket at that time. You put it in your jacket pocket with no more thought given to it. Within a few days you entered Army basic training and AIT thereafter. At any rate, you discover the ticket, check it out, and darned if you aren't holding the winning lotto ticket worth 100 million dollars! The only condition is that you must be in Minneapolis by 9:00 the next morning to claim the winnings. Your home town is Sheridan, Wyoming. Twenty-four hours.

Considerations:
1. You have no auto and your parents' auto needs repairs.
2. You promised the Sheridan hospital that you would drive a cancer patient to Denver, via hospital motor vehicle.
3. You are a pall bearer in two days for the funeral of your best friend's mother. Might be enough time, but could be really tight.
4. Church service/Bible study this evening.

Question: Would any of the above (or anything else) prevent you from making the trip to Minneapolis to claim the 100 million dollars?

<u>Man's view of winning lotto ticket:</u> financial freedom, cars, clothes, the "good life". Minneapolis? <u>I'll be there in time to collect!</u>

<u>God's view of winning lotto ticket:</u> Jesus said: "And what do you benefit if you gain the whole world but lose your own soul? Is anything worth more than your soul?" Mark 8:36-37.

<u>Perseverance is one of God's gifts. Will you use it to save your soul?</u>

Something to think about.

9. WINNING TEAM.

Facts: Each year in professional football there is a SUPER BOWL where the top team in each conference meets to play a championship game. The competition is not restricted to the football game alone. The site of the game, the television and radio broadcasting rights, advertisements, arena capacity, team-shirts, food, beverage, focus of millions. Oh, and did I mention gambling?

Question: Do you think it would be of some "advantage" knowing ahead of time which team is going to win?

Man's view of knowing winning team: Boy, think of the bets I could make; the attention I would get for being "smart" enough to pick the winner; and the comfort I would feel of not having to worry about the outcome.

God's view of knowing winning team: In the "Super Bowl of Life" there are but two teams: The Devil's team and God's team. The two forces are constantly fighting each other (see Galatians 5:17). However, you have access to the book (Bible) that tells you *who* is going to win, and explicitly *how* you can join God's team.

Now, take a moment and let this sink in: You have the comfort of never having to worry about your life's game/spiritual outcome. "If you openly declare that Jesus is LORD (declare belief in Jesus), and believe in your heart that God raised Him from the dead, you *will* be saved." Romans 10:9.

Nothing to think about --- <u>THIS IS A "NO-BRAINER"</u>!

10. If Not Jesus, Who?

Facts: A friend, loved one, or family member is hospitalized --- terminally ill. The doctor said, "Just make him comfortable."

Question: What would you do? Would you pray for wisdom, direction, strength, peace, healing? If so, why?

Could it be that GOD can do things that man cannot? And why not!? Jesus provides healing, faith, and prayer.

"Jesus healed every kind of disease and sickness." Matthew 9:35.

Faith and trust: A woman had suffered bleeding for twelve years. She had heard about Jesus so she came up behind Him and touched His robe, thinking, "If I can touch His robe I will be healed." She did so and was immediately healed. Jesus said, "Daughter, your faith has made you well." Mark 5:25-34. Or, how about the Roman officer whose servant was sick: "Lord I am not worthy that you should come into my home, just say the word, and my servant will be healed." Matthew 8:8.

Prayer: "That is why we never give up. Though our bodies are dying, our spirits are being renewed every day." 2 Corinthians 4:16-17.

There was a time during Jesus' ministry when Jesus was becoming controversial with His teaching, and He asked the disciples if they wanted to leave Him. Simon Peter replied, "Lord, to whom would we go? You have the words that give eternal life. We believe, and we know you are the Holy One of God." John 6:68-69.

Indeed, to whom would you go?

Something to think about.

II. ABORTION.

Facts: recently in the news was the President's nomination to fill a Justice position on the United States Supreme Court. The political parties and the populace were very divided on the nominee's qualifications because of the perceived fear that the 1973 Supreme Court case of Roe vs. Wade might be overturned. Roe vs. Wade allows the killing of an unborn child in certain instances.

Is the Roe vs. Wade decision pertinent to our relationship with GOD?

Man's view: the law of the United States allows abortions.

GOD's view: GOD created the world and man. He gave man an intellect and free will (freedom of choice) plus a standard of conduct. We, as believers, are required to follow GOD's standard of conduct. The Supreme Court of this country cannot, I repeat cannot, give us permission to do something that contravenes (violates, contrary to) GOD's law! Whatever the Supreme Court has previously decided, or will decide, has nothing to do with our relationship with GOD. Following GOD's law has been our individual obligation since our creation.

I find nothing in the scriptures where GOD has given permission to kill an unborn child. Judgment day is between YOU and GOD! It is imperative that you do your own thinking. Overturning Roe vs. Wade --- GOD

20

has already done that by never authorizing it in the first place!

"Preach the word of God. Be prepared, whether the time is favorable or not. Patiently correct, rebuke, and encourage your people with good teaching." 2 Timothy 4:2. Isn't it time to accentuate God's view?

Something to think about.

12. ABORTION AFTERMATH.

I reference my earlier writing regarding abortion, and observations that the Supreme Court of the United States cannot affect *your* personal relationship with GOD; that GOD has not approved the killing of unborn children; and I therefore recommended: do your own thinking.

And what if the decision for an abortion has already been made and performed?

The aftermath can provide long-lasting regret, guilt, and unhappiness. Frankly, this thinking is Spiritually unacceptable to GOD! GOD is all about grace and compassion.

1. Jesus asked for all your burdens and weariness, so you may have rest for your soul (see Matthew 11:28-29).
2. No sin is greater than GOD's forgiveness (see Isaiah 1:18).
3. Paul said forget the past, look forward to the heavenly prize for which GOD, through Jesus Christ, is calling us (see Philippians 3:13-14).
4. GOD forgives and forgets (see Hebrews 8:12). It is His promise!
5. You cannot separate yourself from GODs love (see Romans 8:31-39).

If "aftermath" thinking still haunts you, please think about this:

- Believe that the blood of Jesus covers "all" sins of man?
- If the "aftermath" continues: that thinking is NOT GOD's.
- And for those who may be thinking, "I could have done more," I submit you are speculating that any further effort would have made a difference.
- Further, GOD has already figured that into #4 above.

BOTTOM LINE: If you believe GOD's promises, then you are wrestling with something that no longer exists!

Something to no longer think about!

P.S. Considering the infinite wisdom of GOD, don't you think He has a plan for aborted children? YES, GOD has it figured out.

13. REDEEMER REMINDER.

Facts: You have a four-year-old child whose life was saved by the next-door neighbor boy, by virtue of his courage and sacrifice. You are, obviously, so thankful for the saving of your child and have the utmost respect, gratitude, and love for the neighbor boy. As your child goes through life and reaches certain levels of accomplishment, i.e. eighth grade--high school--college graduation--even higher degrees with continued successes, you are reminded, with each accomplishment, of the "saving" of your child and of your continued joy and love.

And every time you see the neighbor boy, as well as his parents, you are again reminded of how thankful you are for that boy's courage and sacrifice. You think, "I would do most anything to help this boy with his career, etc. This boy will <u>forever</u> be on my mind and in my heart. <u>He saved my child's life! How can I ever forget that? How can I ever show the depth of my love and appreciation?</u>"

Question: Can you identify with the intensity and focus of these feelings and devotion?

<u>God's view:</u> If you are able to have this depth of thankfulness and love for someone who saved your child's life, then what about someone who sacrificed his own life

for the sins and salvation of you and all mankind? <u>Yes,
why not Jesus, with all your mind, heart, soul, and
strength?</u>

John 3:16: "For GOD loved the world so much that he gave
his only Son, so that everyone who believes in him <u>may
not perish</u> but may have eternal life." How can <u>you</u> ever
forget that?

Something to think about --- <u>DAILY!</u>

14. Survivor or Casualty.

Facts: You are on an airplane that crashes in the jungle. Your obvious objective is to make your way through the jungle and back to civilization. No time to waste, you must move forward and address all the obstacles and problems present in any jungle.

Let's go one step further and equate this with your present position in life where your objective is to reach SALVATION (survivor). The "jungle problems" are akin to the tests, trials, tribulations, and obstacles facing us on this earth, including the actions of our fellow man, i.e. jealousy, hatred, discrimination, unlawfulness, greed, exploitation, disrespect, favoritism, inequality, turmoil, etc. And let's not forget about Satan, who works relentlessly to steal our soul -- think about that: Satan is trying to steal your soul and take you to hell with him. (Casualty!)

Question: Can you survive "the jungle of life", and receive salvation? YES --- God shows you the way.

Step 1: Reality: it doesn't make any difference how you got on that airplane or why the plane crashed --- and it makes no difference how you got to where you are today. You are where you are, and that's it. So, forget about the past. Negative occurrences or blaming people from the past is depressive, doesn't solve problems, and doesn't result in changes you may be called upon to make.

Paul gave similar advice over 2000 years ago: "No, dear brothers and sisters I have not achieved perfection, but I FOCUS on this one thing: forgetting the PAST and looking FORWARD to what lies ahead, I press to reach the end of the race and receive the heavenly prize for which GOD, through Jesus Christ is calling us." Philippians 3:13-14.

Step 2 and 3: read next week

15. SURVIVOR OR CASUALTY CONTINUES. (WEEK TWO)

Sit down, take inventory of yourself, and commit to starting "now with GOD". You can't change your beginning, but you can control your ending. Think forward.

Step 2: Become a "believer". Accepting Jesus Christ as your Savior and Lord. You must do and believe the following:

- Acknowledge that you have sinned. Romans 3:23.
- Understand the penalty (wages) for your sins. Romans 6:23.
- Confess and repent of your sins. 1 John 1:9.
- Confess that Jesus Christ is the only way to salvation. John 14:6. Invite and receive Jesus Christ into your life to obtain forgiveness, direction, and eternal life. John 3:3.

You will still have to contend with the trials and tribulations of this world, the actions/omissions of your fellow man, and the ever-working devil. "Do not love this world nor the things it offers you, for when you love the world, you do not have the love of the Father in you. For the world offers only a craving for physical pleasures, a craving for everything we see, and pride in our achievements and possessions. These are NOT from the Father, but are from this world." 1 John 2:15-16.

Step 3: <u>Transition.</u> The transition journey to disregard this world and do what pleases GOD will not be easy. You will need help, so ask for it-- from GOD's church, godly pastors, family, or friends. Be comforted in knowing you <u>cannot</u> separate yourself from GOD's love, and GOD does not test you beyond your strength to endure. Jesus said, "<u>Take heart because I have overcome the world!</u>" John 16:33.

You were created to be a survivor. START NOW.

Something to think about.

16. THREE STRIKES AND YOU'RE OUT.

Facts: "And it's one, two, three strikes you're out, at the 'ole ball game." Do you remember that baseball song? GOD also has "three strikes". The trinity consists of (1) GOD the Father, (2) GOD the Son, and (3) GOD the Holy Spirit.

GOD the Father gave us the ten commandments, the prophets, and Jesus. GOD the Son---Jesus---became man, died for our sins, rose from the dead, is alive today, and gives us the opportunity for SALVATION. And, when Jesus ascended to heaven, He left us GOD the Holy Spirit. GOD the Holy Spirit resides within the believer and is available for spiritual guidance, support, and assistance daily. "Don't you realize that your body is the temple (home) of the Holy Spirit, who lives in you and was given to you by GOD?" 1 Corinthians 6:19.

Question: Is there a possible correlation between a baseball game, the Trinity, and salvation?

Man's View: A baseball game and, after three strikes, you're out.

GOD's View:
Rejecting God the Father is strike one.

Rejecting GOD the Son is strike two.

Rejecting GOD the Holy Spirit is <u>strike three.</u>

This isn't a ballgame, rather life. And, if you committed the above "strikes", you have rejected heaven for hell. And here's the irony: <u>GOD MADE YOU YOUR OWN UMPIRE!</u>

Something to think about.

P.S. GOD did not create you to strike out!

17. Salvation Deadline?

Facts: many daily transactions have "time" deadlines, i.e., guarantees, warranties, repaying loans, items "on sale", and others. When Jesus died on the cross, He was flanked by two thieves. Luke 23: 39-43 provides: "One of the criminals hanging beside him scoffed. 'So you're the Messiah, are you? Prove it by saving yourself—and us too, while you're at it.' But the other criminal protested, 'Don't you fear GOD even when you have been sentenced to die? We deserve to die for our crimes, but this man hasn't done anything wrong; then <u>he said, 'Jesus remember me when you come into your Kingdom.' And Jesus replied, 'I assure you today you will be with me in paradise.'"</u>

Question: Is there a time-table for SALVATION?

The length of time for the exchange between the penitent thief and Jesus may have been just seconds. A short moment of repentance and confession, and Jesus assured the criminal of eternal life in paradise (heaven). Unlike the purchase of a new vehicle with a warranty subject to expiration, <u>there is no time limit on GOD's guarantees and promises, as long as we confess, are truly sorry, and accept this gracious gift.</u>

I was told a story about a man who died, went to heaven, and while visiting with GOD, asked GOD if it is true that His capacity for mercy and forgiveness has no limit, to which GOD said "yes". Then the man asked, "If that is true, why didn't You forgive Satan?" And GOD replied, "HE NEVER ASKED!" No time limit, just ask!

Something to think about.

Author's Caution: I WOULDN'T WAIT UNTIL I AM HANGING FROM A CROSS TO MAKE THE PLEA!

Jesus looked at them intently and said, "Humanly speaking, it is impossible. But with God everything is possible."
Matthew 19:26

Graphic from the YouVersion Bible app

18. ACE IN THE HOLE.

Defined as someone or something to fall back upon, especially when faced with adversity; a security blanket; a life-saver. So, what is your "ace in the hole"? Might it depend on how you view the world, i.e. GOD's view — or Man's view? If man's view, you might think your ace in the hole is an extra $20,000 in a bank account, a friend or acquaintance in a "high position", or family connections. If you think GOD's view, you think Jesus! The crux is whether your concern is for this life or the next!

Think about it, every person who has ever lived on this earth with great wealth, vast empires, power, influence — left it all here when they passed! Focus on your next life, and ask yourself:

- Who died for your sins and rose from the dead so you can have eternal life?
- Whose behavior should you follow to enter the Kingdom?
- Whose forgiveness exceeds your gravest sin?
- When observing a human tragedy, have you ever blurted out, "Oh, my GOD!"? The reason is Jesus lives inside of you — allow yourself to live in Jesus.

Earthly life is an adversity-------Jesus *is* your "ace in the hole."

Plenty to think about.

19. FORGIVENESS: THE TOUGHEST TEST OF LOVE?

Facts: in June, 2015 in Charleston, South Carolina, a 21-year old white supremacist walked into the Emanuel African Methodist Episcopal Church and murdered nine church members. Reason? HATE. Remarkably, several family members of those killed expressed FORGIVENESS of the murderer. (It is one of the greatest examples of racial healing in my lifetime, yet unheralded by the press.)

Question: does GOD expect this kind of forgiveness?

"Since GOD chose you to be the holy people He loves, you must clothe yourselves with tenderhearted mercy, kindness, humility, gentleness, and patience. Make allowance for each other's faults and <u>forgive anyone who offends you. Remember, the Lord forgave you, so you must forgive others.</u> Above all, clothe yourselves with <u>LOVE</u>, which binds us all together in perfect harmony. And let the <u>peace</u> that comes from <u>Christ</u> rule in your hearts." Colossians 3:12-15. You will note there is no mention of race, creed, or color as it relates to forgiveness.

Your forgiveness provides three positives: (1) clears out your bitterness and possible hatred; (2) may produce a positive in the person being forgiven when he sees you have forgiven him; and (3) you are showing the world that GOD lives within you, and praise will be given to your heavenly Father.

If you love as GOD loves, then other people's behavior does not detract from that love. With love, <u>forgiveness is automatic and given without being asked.</u>

Something to think about.

20. LAST CHANCE CONVERSATION.

Could the most important day in your life be <u>the day you die?</u> This is your day of judgment. "For we must all stand before Christ to be judged. We will each receive whatever we deserve for the good or evil we have done in this earthly body." 2 Corinthians 5:10.

<u>Facts:</u> Here's the scene: You have died and find yourself in a waiting room. You are comfortable, yet anxious and apprehensive. An Angel approaches, "JESUS WILL BE WITH YOU SHORTLY." You impulsively ask, "Do you have a Bible I might use?"

As you sit awaiting your visit with GOD (through Jesus, the Son), many thoughts at the <u>speed of light</u> pass through your mind, i.e. your sins, regrets, unforgiveness, disrespect, unfairness, inequality, lies, deceit, discrimination, hatred----all your dealings with your fellow man. All this, as well as the admonition of Jesus: "Love one another, as I have loved you."

Wow, I hadn't really planned for this time, <u>at this time;</u> I sure hope He's in a good mood! Your heart pounds as you come to this FULL REALIZATION: "Nothing in all creation is hidden from GOD. Everything is naked and exposed before His eyes, and He is the one to whom we are accountable." Hebrews 4:13.

The Angel returns, "Jesus will see you now."

Question: What do you say to Jesus, as your last chance conversation?

Before you can speak, Jesus speaks: <u>"I know when you failed me.</u>

<u>"Can you tell me when I failed you?"</u>

Something to think about -- and plan ahead.

21. LIVING EQUALITY.

<u>Facts:</u> You are attending a football game between Michigan and Ohio State in Ann Arbor, Michigan. There are 100,000 fans there. Football players, coaches, presidents from each university, students, families, fans, band, clean-up crews, maintenance people, sports-writers, people with wealth, position, social recognition; in short, people from "all walks of life".

<u>Question:</u> Can you view "equality" through GOD's view of the world?

Equality is a <u>promise</u> from GOD. He has no favorites (see 1 Peter 1:17). We all are <u>ONE</u> in Christ Jesus. We all have individual skills so we can work in harmony with each other. No person is more important than another, and we need one another to function as GOD intended (see 1 Corinthians Chapter 12).

Since GOD is the "<u>Great Equalizer</u>", we should feel neither inferiority nor superiority with our fellow beings. Feeling inferior is often the result of our perception that others have "more" or are "more important". Yet, why do we feel inferior if GOD views us as equals? Trust GOD and have faith in His word. <u>In GOD's eyes, you will never meet a person on this earth who is MORE important than you!</u>

Equality also excludes <u>superiority</u>. We want to be treated equally, but what about our attitude, love, and treatment of *others?* We have an obligation to help our fellow man. "Lord, when did we ever see you hungry or thirsty or a stranger or naked or sick or in prison, and <u>not</u> help you? <u>I tell you the truth, when you refused to help the least of these, my brothers and sisters, you were refusing to help me.</u>" Matthew 25:44-45. Jesus is present in *every* human being. If you refuse those who need help, you are refusing Jesus! <u>In GOD's eyes, you will never meet a person on this earth who is less important than you!</u>

Something to think about it.

P.S. And what about the guy who sits at a highway intersection with a sign, "broke, hungry, out of work veteran?" Mother Theresa: "If you are honest and sincere people may deceive you. <u>Be honest and sincere anyway!</u>" Further, the person asking may NOT be deceiving you and may honestly need your help.

22. FAILURE TO COMMUNICATE.

In the 1967 movie, "Cool Hand Luke", Paul Neuman portrays a prison inmate in Florida. He is rebellious, deceitful, disrespectful, unforgiving, unreligious, arrogant, and self-centered. Yet in his fellow prisoners' eyes, <u>Luke is "cool"</u>. He refuses to conform to the prison rules. He runs off from work details on several occasions which results in grave punishment, restrictions, and ultimate death. Among the several quotes, the most unforgettable for me is when the captain of the prison guards addresses the men after an incident of rule-breaking, exclaiming, "<u>What we've got here is FAILURE TO COMMUNICATE.</u>"

GOD gave us Moses and 10 commandments, the prophets, His son Jesus, thereafter the disciples (including Paul), the scriptures, the four gospels, a new covenant, left us with the Holy Spirit, daily invitations, and daily reminders to pray and be strong so we will enjoy His promise of eternal life.

<u>Hardly a "failure to communicate"</u>!

GOD is waiting for you to pray. Jesus (see Matthew 6:5-15) taught you how to pray, commonly referred to as the "Our Father or the Lord's Prayer". Prayer allows you to express your praise, your needs, your thanks, your forgiveness, your concerns, and your worries. Prayer allows you to walk with Jesus and <u>save your soul.</u>

Question: "Cool" from Luke ---- or "soul-saving"
communication with GOD?

Jesus has a standing invitation: "Look, I stand at the door
and knock. <u>If you hear my voice and open the door, I will
come in, and we will share a meal together as friends.</u>"
Revelation 3:20.

<u>PLEASE DON'T WAIT ANY LONGER TO INVITE
JESUS IN.</u>

P.S. The communication need not be scripted---just
speak from your heart. (Example): "Lord, Jesus, I come
to you because I desperately need your help. Too often, I
feel this world is squeezing me to conform to its ways.
Help me avoid this world and assist me in not letting me
slip back into my old way of living, rather, I pray to be
"reborn" in you. I know I cannot do this on my own. . . . .
. . . <u>Communicate daily using your own words.</u>

<u>Plenty to think about.</u>

23. THE DEVIL MADE ME DO IT.

Do you remember that saying from the Flip Wilson television show? Understand that the words "do it" mean actions outside the standard of conduct set by GOD. The phrase may have been a statement of intended levity, but its implications are not a laughing matter. Scriptures reveal the spiritual death of Satan:

- A. Satan, the one deceiving the whole world, was thrown from heaven, down to earth with all his angels (now demons) (see Revelation:12:9).
- B. Woe to the inhabitants of earth since the devil has great wrath and knows he has but a short time (see Revelation 12:12).
- C. The world around us is controlled by the evil one (see 1 John 5:19).
- D. "Stay alert! Watch out for your great enemy, the devil. He prowls around like a roaring lion, looking for someone to devour. Stand firm against him and be strong in your faith." 1 Peter 5: 8-9.
- E. Satan is destined for hell to be tormented forever (see Revelation 20:10).

Scriptures tell us Satan has already been defeated by the death and resurrection of Jesus Christ, but Satan has retained his deceit and trickery to convince <u>you</u> to relinquish <u>your salvation earned through the blood of Jesus.</u>

Satan Alert! "The devil doesn't come dressed in a red cape and pointy horns. <u>He comes as everything you've ever wished for!</u>" (Tucker Max). This is precisely why you should not love this world nor the things it offers you. Cravings for physical pleasures, for everything you see, pride in your achievements and possessions---<u>are all from this world</u> (see 1 John 2:15-16).

"Flip" gives you an <u>excuse (the Devil).</u>

GOD gives you <u>protection from the excuse!</u> "But the Lord is faithful; He will strengthen you and guard you from the <u>evil one.</u>" 2 Thessalonians 3:3.

Something to think about.

P.S. You can't blame your choices on the devil, and you know it.

24. I AM THE GREATEST!

Heavyweight boxer Muhammed Ali said that. In fact, he said it more than once! It was self-designated but did generate much discussion and argument. Who was the "greatest" in golf, basketball, baseball, hockey, football, leader, intellect, author, the greatest teams in sports, etc.? Often, we bestow adulation and seemingly infinite discussion about the earthly accomplishments of our fellow man. Praise and perceived importance are frequently sought in an attempt to be the "greatest" — yet another accolade from "man's view" of this world.

Even the apostles argued who was the greatest among them, at the Last Supper. "Then they began to argue among themselves about who would be the greatest among them. Jesus told them, 'In this world the kings and great men lord it over their people, yet they are called friends of the people. But among you it will be different. Those who are the greatest among you shall take the lowest rank, and the leader should be like a servant.... "For I am among you as one who serves." Luke 22:24-27. "For even the Son of man came not to be served but to serve others and to give his life as a ransom for many." Matthew 20:28.

Paul, in his letter to Titus wrote: "Our people must learn to do good by meeting the urgent needs of others; then they will not be unproductive." Titus 3:14.

The urgent needs of others may also be spiritual.

"And you must show mercy to those whose faith is wavering. Rescue others by snatching them from the flames of judgement." Jude 22-23

Are you the greatest (servant) you can be?

Something to think about.

P.S. I have done some reading about those people who are in hospice or elsewhere knowing they will die soon. One of the most prevalent thoughts or regrets among them is "I wish I had done more for others." If you are NOT yet one of these dying people, then *there is still time.*

More to think about.

"No one can read the Gospels without feeling the actual presence of Jesus. His personality pulsates in every word. No myth is filled with such life." Albert Einstein

25. EINSTEIN FOR JESUS.

I am sure most of us are familiar with Albert Einstein, a world-renowned expert in physics and mathematics. During his life, he was often considered the smartest man in the world. Einstein once stated: "Try not to be a man of success, but rather try to be become a man of value."

Jesus told us a man of "value" renders his life assisting others, i.e. the hungry, the thirsty, the homeless, the poor, the sick, the naked, the prisoner, the weak, being a friend, (see Matthew 25:35-40), and inspiring others to do the same (see Hebrews 10:24).

Conclusion: the smartest man in the world thought like Jesus!

Something to think about.

26. The Condition of Your Condition!

Even in a courtroom, amusing incidents occur. One such instance occurred when I was hearing a case regarding child visitation. The father suffered from a bipolar disorder so I had to be assured that he could, by himself, properly supervise his two children. A letter from a physician would support the father's capability to have unsupervised visitation rights. So, I set a further hearing giving the father opportunity to bring the requested letter. Two weeks later in a continued hearing, I asked the father if he had the requested letter. The father said, "No, your honor, I didn't have time <u>to find out what condition my condition was in.</u>" I couldn't help but smile.

But, I encourage you to concentrate on the condition of your condition---your "spiritual condition". We all have interests, habits, occupations, or any number of different activities demanding our daily attention. God wants us to enjoy the world He gave us. However, our spiritual condition, our relationship with God, is paramount. We know the Lord will come as a thief in the night. We must be ready (see 1 Thessalonians 5:2).

Read the Scriptures and learn how to be ready. If you are NOT ready, <u>get ready</u>! If you ARE ready then don't slip back into your old ways of living to satisfy your own desires, rather "remain in the fellowship with Christ so that when He returns, you will be full of courage and not shrink back from Him in shame." 1 John 2:28.

We "remain in fellowship with Christ" by remaining faithful to His teachings. We should pray throughout the day (see 1 Thessalonians 5:17) Perhaps you can exercise daily morning prayers, daily meditation with God, daily Scripture reading, or memorize a Scripture verse to fortify you when needed, a quick prayer of thanks during the day -- or pray at bedtime. But, always pray in Jesus' name.

Then you *will* be "ready" and full of courage and confidence when Jesus returns.

Something to think about.

27. LOST AND FOUND.

Facts: A toddler (two-three years) is shopping with mom in a modern mall. Something catches the child's eye, leading to time spent examining the item. A short time later the child turns away from the item and mom is nowhere to be seen. LOST! A nice, caring shopper tries to console the now crying child, but the niceness received from another is <u>pale in comparison</u> to the love, comfort, and security of <u>mom</u>. Soon, a frantic-looking lady breaks through the surrounding strangers, her unrelenting search is over yes, ------ it's mom! Nothing else matters; child and mom are <u>reunited;</u> comfort, love and security return.

During high school or college years, during initial working years when employment performance and advancement are paramount, during the involvement in sports, social gatherings, graduations, tragedies like divorce, death of a loved one, addictions, war, or the bustle of worldly life, one can be distracted and "lose" GOD. Your relationship with GOD can be interrupted or become just a robotic act of habitual religious commitment, lacking the love GOD expects.

Issue: Do you feel lost?

We have learned from the Bible that we lose our needed contact with GOD when we think only about life here on earth, while we should be thinking about Godly things of heaven. Sometimes you can feel so disorientated that you have no confidence in your ability to turn away from this world and back to the Lord.

Solution: <u>Reunite</u> with God's love. After all, <u>He didn't lose you!</u> "The Son of Man came to <u>seek and save those who are lost.</u>" Luke 19:10.

Jesus is standing at your door knocking. Open the door and He will come in and share a meal together as friends (see Revelation 3:20). The person who died for your sins and rose from the dead for your salvation, is asking to come into, and <u>remain</u> in your life. Jesus makes it so easy to no longer be lost!

<u>The lost is found!</u>

Something to think about.

28. UNFATHOMABLE.

This is defined as incapable of being fully explored or understood.

"Do you not know? Have you not heard? The Lord is the everlasting GOD, the Creator of the ends of the earth. <u>He will not grow tired or weary, and his 'understanding' no one can fathom.</u>" Isaiah 40:28. (Old Testament).

"Oh, how great are GOD's riches and wisdom and knowledge! <u>How impossible it is for us to understand his decisions and his ways.</u>" Romans 11:33.

"And may you have the power to understand, as all GOD's people should, how wide, how long, how high, and how deep His love is. May you experience the love of Christ, <u>though it is too great to understand fully.</u>" Ephesians 3:18-19.

"No power in the sky above or in the earth below--- indeed, <u>nothing in all creation</u> will ever be able to separate us from the love of GOD that is revealed in Christ Jesus our Lord." Romans 8:38.

"No eye has seen, no ear has heard, and no mind has imagined what GOD has prepared for those who love him." 1 Corinthians 2:9.

Let's review:

- His understanding is <u>unfathomable.</u>
- His decisions and ways are <u>unfathomable.</u>
- The width, length, height, and depth of His love is <u>unfathomable.</u>
- His love is inseparable and forever. <u>Unfathomable.</u>
- What GOD has prepared for us who love him is <u>unfathomable.</u>
- GOD <u>forgives and forgets</u> (see Hebrews 8:12). <u>Unfathomable.</u>

Don't waste your time trying to comprehend the unfathomable. You simply don't have the brain power. Spend your time praising and thanking GOD daily for <u>His unfathomable, selfless, saving gifts</u>, earned for <u>you</u> through the shed blood of Jesus.

Something to think *and* pray about.

29. Don't Put the Cart Before the Horse.

The above phrase is generally defined as doing things in the wrong order.

Lives are often spent somewhat in the following order: learning obedience as a child; being educated; employment considerations; perhaps marriage and children; and then filled with "busy-ness" until we retire from our employment. During retirement you might make a more concentrated effort to learn about GOD, the Bible, our Savior Jesus Christ, and salvation.

Is focusing on salvation at life's end putting the "cart before the horse"?

Scripture provides that we should know and accept the following:
1. GOD had a plan for ALL before He made the world. He chose you to be in His family and brought to Him through Jesus Christ (see Ephesians 1:4-5).
2. GOD wants you to be saved. (see 1 Timothy 2-3) --- from eternal torment.
3. Jesus died for your sins, rose from the dead, and lives today, to offer you eternal life (see Romans 5:8-11).

4. Seek the Kingdom of GOD above all else (see Matthew 6:33).
5. The reward for trusting Jesus is the salvation of your soul (see 1 Peter 1:9).

GOD's first thought in His plan for ALL (you), is salvation! Shouldn't salvation be the first thought and driving force in your life? ABSOLUTELY!
1 Thessalonians 5:16-18 provides that we should always be joyful, never stop praying, and be thankful in all circumstances, in accordance with GOD's will. You might ask: "How is this possible in today's world?"

You can do this because you know your salvation has been planned by GOD, your forgiveness earned through the blood of Jesus, and as a "believer" in the death and resurrection of Jesus, eternal and peaceful life (salvation) is promised and waiting for you.

Salvation is your planned destination, and your daily motivation!

It is the "horse" for your cart.

Something to think about.

30. QUIT COMPLAINING AND DO WHAT I SAY!

Have you ever heard this *from* a parent? Have you ever said this *as* a parent?

This usually occurs because the parent has dictated a plan that has not been followed, and the parent is sure that, if followed, the child will develop personal responsibility, accountability, knowledge, respect and honesty.

The Scriptures tell us, in no uncertain terms, that GOD, our all-knowing parent, has a dictated "plan" for each of us. We do not follow it, but we do complain, i.e. why does GOD allow bad things to happen? Why didn't GOD create me "better"? Couldn't life be easier? That's not fair!

Have you ever read or heard this: It's better not to "bail" someone out of their challenge; they will be a better person if they have to "work their way through it"!

Jesus did not promise you a carefree and easy life. In fact, Jesus told you just the opposite---there would be many trials and sorrows (see John 16:33). But these trials and sorrows are NOT the proper subject of complaining, rather a proper subject that you have the perseverance and the strength to overcome and demonstrate that your faith is genuine. "My grace is all you need. My power works best in weakness." 2 Corinthians 12:9.

"Do everything without complaining and arguing, so that no one can criticize you. Live clean, innocent lives as children of God, shining like bright lights in a world full of crooked and perverse people." Philippians 2:14-15.

<u>Facts:</u> God is the reason you exist; God has a plan of salvation for you; God sent His Son to teach you how to endear yourself to Him and to your fellow-man; God loves you so much He sent His Son to die for your sins; God raised His Son from the dead so you might have eternal life; God will assist you whenever you ask. *You have nothing to complain about!*

If you do complain and your complaining results in <u>not doing what God says</u>, then you are not only disappointing God, but making Satan really happy.

Something to think about

31. I WANT THE TRUTH -- YOU CAN'T HANDLE THE TRUTH!

This was a verbal exchange between Tom Cruise and Jack Nicholson in the movie, "A Few Good Men". Tom Cruise: "I want the truth!" Jack Nicholson: "You can't handle the truth!" Just lines in a movie, or a spiritual reality?

Salvation is your reward for trusting in Jesus, who stated the following:

TRUTH: "I am the way, the truth, and the life. No one can come to the Father except through me." John 14:6.

LOVE: Love GOD, with your whole mind, heart, and soul; love your neighbor as yourself ("neighbor" includes your enemies) (see Matthew 22:37-39).

KINGDOM: "Seek the Kingdom of GOD above all else, and live righteously, and he will give you everything you need." Matthew 6:33.

WILL OF GOD: "And this is the will of GOD, that I should not lose even one of all those he has given me, but that I should raise them up at the last day. For this is my Father's will that all who see his Son and believe in him should have eternal life. I will raise them up at the last day." John 6:38-40.

SERVITUDE: "For even the Son of Man came not to be served but to serve others...." Matthew 20:28.

LIFE: "If any of you wants to be my follower, you must turn from your selfish ways, take up your cross, and follow me. If you try to hang onto your life, you will lose it. But if you give up your life for my sake, you will save it." Matthew 16:24-25.

PROMISE: "And be sure of this, I am with you always, even to the end of the age." Matthew 28:20.

Jesus IS the truth. You must want, accept, and live the "truth". Can you handle the truth?

Something to think about.

32. REFUSING THE WORD AND JESUS.

The Word: the Lord said to Moses, "How long will these people treat me with contempt? How long will they refuse to believe in me, in spite of all the miraculous signs I have performed among them?" Numbers 14:11. (Old Testament.)

Jesus: "If GOD were your Father, you would love me, because I have come to you from GOD. I am not here on my own, but He sent me. Why can't you understand what I am saying? It's because you can't even hear me! For you are the children of your father the devil, and you love to do the evil things he does." There is no truth in Satan, "So when I tell you the truth, you just naturally don't believe me! Anyone who belongs to GOD listens gladly to the words of GOD. But you don't listen because you don't belong to GOD." John 8:42-45. "And you do not have His message in your hearts, because you do not believe me---the one He sent to you." John 5:38. Does Jesus sound frustrated? Jesus died for our sins and does not deserve frustration.

Believe The Evidence: "But I have a greater witness than John (the Baptist) -- My teachings and My miracles. The Father gave me these works to accomplish, and they prove that He sent me." John 5:36. "Don't believe me unless I carry out my Father's work. But if I do His work, believe in the evidence of the *miraculous works I have done*, even if you don't believe Me. Then you will know and understand that the Father is in Me, and I am in the Father." John 10:37-38.

Living in this day and age, the "truth" of GOD's Word, the teaching, and miracles of Jesus are readily available for learning and following. The Bible is the only book we need to discover how to know and walk with GOD. Read the Bible, be "reborn" with Christ in your heart, and continually seek the protection of GOD until you receive His promised salvation of your soul.

GOD's Guarantee: It is often easy to refuse something with which you are unfamiliar. If you "invest" your GOD-given life to learn and accept GOD's "Word" and Jesus, you will NEVER refuse them! The "return" on your investment is the Kingdom of GOD for eternity. This is GOD's guarantee.

Something to think about.

33. Ship of Fools.

WELCOME ABOARD!

You have the journey of your every dream. A virtual extravaganza of delights. No unhappiness or inhibitions allowed. Life is not to be endured, rather lived to the fullest---you only go around once! There is nothing as important as your enjoyment of life. This is Las Vegas on the water, whatever happens here, stays here! <u>Cruise as long as you like.</u> And to assist, we have:

Luxury accommodations
Food
Alcohol
Gambling
Mood altering substances
Exotic dancers
Dating service
Movies
Dances
Party the night away evenings
Shows
Prizes, gifts
Memories ---- and more!

Name of the Ship: Hell-Bound.
Cruise director: Satan. (in the form of everything you've ever wished for!)

"They traded the truth about GOD for a lie. <u>So, they worshipped and served the things GOD created instead of the Creator himself.</u>" Romans 1:25. "Claiming to be wise, <u>they, instead, became UTTER FOOLS.</u>" Romans 1:22.

"And I will be your Father, and you will be my sons and daughters says the Lord Almighty." 2 Corinthians 6:18.

You are not a fool but rather a "child of GOD."

Something to think about.

Repent. Come home!

34. Don't Miss the Opportunity to Strike While the Iron Is Hot.

God's spiritual opportunity is for us to accept Jesus as our redeemer and savior and receive Him into the very core of our lives. Jesus Christ alone leads you to God. (see John 14:6). The opportunity is given to you <u>daily</u> by His knocking on your door; all you have to do is open it, and say, Jesus, come in"! (see Revelation 3:20). However, God's opportunity also includes the requirement of true and genuine repentance of sins ----a kind of repentance that leads you away from sin and results in salvation (see 2 Corinthians 7:10).

Judas, the betrayer, who turned Jesus over to be crucified, failed because he had remorse only -- without repentance (see Matthew 27:3), and <u>missed his opportunity.</u>

And, let's not forget the <u>near miss</u> by the thief on the cross next to Jesus; a whisper away from death, yet he repented, accepted Jesus, and was saved -- "to be with Jesus in paradise."

Don't be a "missed" or "near miss". <u>Repent,</u> and rest your soul with Jesus NOW! God's iron is always "hot", waiting for you to "strike", and come home.

Something to think about.

35. DEAD INSIDE.

I, too, spin through the TV channels looking for entertainment. Sometimes, I "land" on a channel depicting people slowly staggering around, clothes torn, deformed faces, mindless, and usually at nighttime. I did not continue watching the channel but became curious, so I did some research. The TV Series is "The Walking Dead". It started playing in 2010 (still playing) and the story entails survivors of a zombie apocalypse. Seeing these zombies called "walkers" reminded me of myself when I did not have Jesus in my life. Of course, I had a brain, but it was registering with my sinful nature and not spiritual matters.

"Once you were DEAD because of your disobedience and your many sins. You used to live in sin, just like the rest of the world, obeying the devil---the commander of the powers in the unseen world. He is the spirit at work in the hearts of those who refuse to obey God. All of us used to live that way, following the passionate desires and inclinations of our sinful nature. By our very nature we were subject to God's anger, just like everyone else." Ephesians 2:1-3.

"But God is so rich in mercy and he loved us so much, that even though we were DEAD because of our sins, he gave us life when he raised Christ from the dead. (It is only by God's grace that you have been saved!) For he raised us from the dead along with Christ and seated us with him in the heavenly realms because we are united with Christ Jesus. So God can point to us in all future ages as examples of the incredible wealth of his grace and kindness toward us, as shown in all he has done for us who are united with Christ Jesus." Ephesians 2:4-7.

"For the wages of sin is death, <u>but the free gift of God is eternal life through Christ Jesus our Lord.</u>" Romans 6:23. Jesus spoke: "I am the light of the world. If you follow me, you won't have to walk in darkness, because you will have the light that leads to life." John 8:12.

You are no longer "mindless" for your spiritual needs; you have the light; and you are welcomed as a "child of God". Kick out the darkness, the devil, and the zombie with him! Welcome to salvation.

Something to think about.

36. THE BULLPEN.

The bullpen is the area where relief pitchers "warm up" before entering a baseball game. When a pitcher develops his skills sufficiently and earns the <u>trust</u> of his coach, he will be called to go in and <u>save the game.</u>

You too, have a "bullpen" where you "warm up" until you earn the <u>trust and approval</u> of your coach and He says you are ready to enter the Kingdom. Your "bullpen" incudes personal struggles of your sinful nature; your dealings with the sinful nature of your fellow man (see Galatians 5:19); and Satan. If you are still in your bullpen, never stop praying ---- <u>visit with and listen to your coach!</u>

Spiritually emerging from the "bullpen" is when you confess and repent your sins (see 1 John 1:9), believe that Jesus is your only way to salvation (see John 14:6), receive Jesus into your life and be "reborn" (see John 3:3), have assurance of your salvation and intimacy with your Savior (see 1 Peter 1:3-5), and are called out of your bullpen to enter the eternal paradise.

Question: What, and where, is the help I need to emerge from my "bullpen"?

Answer: <u>THE BIBLE (word of God) and JESUS (your salvation).</u>

YOUR TEAM:

Infield: Matthew, Mark, Luke, and John.
Outfield: Peter, Paul and James.
Battery: Pitcher is Jesus; Catcher is GOD the Father.
Coach: GOD the Holy Spirit for daily support and guidance.
Bench: GOD's Angels.

AND JESUS IS THROWING THE ONLY PITCH HE KNOWS---LOVE & COMPASSION!

The word of GOD and the love of Jesus conquers everything in your "bullpen"!

I am not trying to be cute. Your winning team is <u>real and available</u> at all times. Yet, some refuse to join.

<u>Remorse can last forever!</u>

Something to think about.

Plaque and photo from Jolene Roth -- SweetlyBundled.com

37. EXPERT ADVICE AND ASSISTANCE.

In life, many people who want to excel in their endeavors of interest will contact experts to advise and assist, i.e., sports like golf, singing, sewing, culinary skills, house painting, etc. They spend money and time learning to be the "best they can be".

You strive Spiritually to "be the best you can be", too, and the proper way to do this is to check in with the *real* experts, <u>The Father, The Son, and The Holy Spirit.</u> They are in your Bible, have unchallenged qualifications, have the best advice possible, and each year they are rated #1. Plus, the instruction doesn't cost you "one thin dime"!

You can't get into heaven by being a good golfer, but you can by being a good and faithful servant (see Matthew 25:23). The Bible -- be the best you can be.

Something to think about.

38. LOVE CONQUERS ALL.

"All You Need Is Love." It's a tune by the Beatles music quartet. "Nothing you can do, that can't be done; no one you can save, that can't be saved. It's easy. All you need is love." Words in a song, not only to be sung, but lived—by GOD's grace.

You cannot separate yourself from GOD's love (see Romans 8:38-39). On the other hand, you must stay separated from the influence of Satan's hate!

Concerning Satan, Jesus said, "He was a murderer from the beginning. He has always hated the truth, because there is no truth in him. When he lies, it is consistent with his character; for he is a liar and the father of lies." John 8:44. Satan hates GOD and all people who praise, promote, and believe in GOD. Therefore, Satan hates you! Satan is pure deceit, and his entire purpose in life is the convince you he cares enough (he doesn't) so you might follow him to certain eternal, tormented death.

"We know how much GOD loves us, and we have put our trust in His love. GOD is love, and all who live in love live in GOD, and GOD lives in them. And as we live in GOD, our love grows more perfect. So we will not be afraid on the day of judgment, but we can face him with confidence because we live like Jesus here in this world. Such love has no fear, because perfect love expels all fear. If we are afraid, it is for fear of punishment, and this shows that we have not fully experienced his perfect love." I John 4:16 and 18.

Let me digest the aforementioned verses: When you <u>trust and experience</u> GOD's perfect love, you will no longer fear Satan, punishment, living, dying, earthly trials and tribulations --- Love <u>expels all fear</u> --- as well as <u>Satan-induced hatred.</u> Further, GOD's commandments are not burdensome when you love GOD (see I John 5:3).

It appears the Beatles were right: love *is* all you need.

Something to think about.

P.S. An "unofficial" poll of those in hell shows that <u>not one wants to stay!</u>

39. BODY OR SOUL.

A married couple in their 60s discover that the wife has breast cancer and the husband has lung cancer, both in an advanced stage. After visiting with their physician, they learn the treatment and side effects on their "road to bodily survival": there is surgery, radiation, chemotherapy, hormone therapy, even stem cell transplant procedures. Side effects can include hair loss, mouth sores, loss of appetite, nausea and vomiting, increased chances of infection, fatigue, anemia (reduced number of red blood cells), bleeding, pain and discomfort. They can last months or even years. Further, the treatments can go on for many months and sometimes years only to have the cancer return. Most people do not hesitate to choose and follow an outlined, potentially life saving treatment procedure, irrespective of the time, effort, pain, discomfort, monetary cost, and perseverance involved.

During our lives we choose diets, exercise, surgical procedures, hairdressers, hair pieces, clothes, skin creams, spas, and other behavior designed to complement our bodies and prolong our earthly life.

Question: What of your soul?

We care how we look. GOD does not! GOD looks at your heart, not your outward appearance (see 1 Samuel 16:7). "Physical training is good, but training for Godliness is much better, promising benefits in this life and in the life to come." 1 Timothy 4:7-8.

Listen up! GOD didn't create you to watch you die, or so you could focus on being a good-looking corpse! Your salvation is what's paramount. Jesus asks you, "Is anything worth more than your soul?" Mark 8:37.

Wake up and smell the roses before they put them on your casket!

Something to think about.

40. KISS (Keep It Simple, Stupid).

KISS was a design principle, adopted by the United States Navy in 1960, that most systems work best if they are kept simple rather than made complicated. Simplicity is a key goal – in design *and* life.

Christianity's "KISS":

1. Don't use your freedom to satisfy your sinful nature, instead use your freedom to serve one another in love. The Holy Spirit produces love, joy, peace, patience, kindness, goodness, faithfulness, gentleness, and self-control in your lives. Let the Holy Spirit be your guide so you won't be doing evil in accordance with your sinful nature (see Galatians 5:13, 16, & 22-23).
2. The Spirit is God's guarantee that He will give you the inheritance He promised and that He has purchased us as His own (see Ephesians 1:14).
3. You cannot separate yourself from God's love (see Romans 8:39).
4. No sin is greater than God's promised forgiveness (see Hebrews 8:12).
5. "You must have the same attitude that Christ Jesus had." Philippians 2:5

God has made following Jesus "KISS".

Are you going to adopt the "kiss" of Christianity or kiss it good-bye?

Something to think about.

41. GOD'S SILVER LINING.

Facts: In 1873, Horatio Stafford, a devout Christian, sent his wife and four daughters on the French ocean liner, Ville du Havre, from the United States to Europe. Their ship collided with another ship and all four of his daughters perished, but his wife survived. In all, 226 people died.

As Horatio was traveling to Europe on another ship to reunite with his wife, he wrote the verse, "It Is Well with My Soul". In 1876, composer Philip Bliss set it to music. First Stanza:
"When peace like a river, attendeth my way,
When sorrows like sea billows roll;
Whatever my lot, Thou hast taught,
It is well, it is well, with my soul. "

Boat (and other modes of transportation) crashes are a part of life. GOD certainly didn't cause the tragedy and He could have left it as is, but GOD inspired Horatio to write a song that <u>serves all of us well today---whatever our lot--- at any given time.</u> "Whatever my lot, Thou hast taught, It is well, it *is* well, with my soul."

What a strength-giving song. We will not buckle nor be intimidated under the rigors of this imperfect life.

Scripture provides a similar message. "This is why we <u>never give up.</u> Though our bodies are dying, <u>our spirits</u>

are being renewed each day. For our present troubles are small and won't last very long. Yet they produce for us a glory that vastly outweighs them and will last forever! So, we don't look at the troubles we can see now; rather, we fix our gaze on things that cannot be seen. For the things we see now will soon be gone, but the things we cannot see will last forever." 2 Corinthians 4:16-18.

The inspired writing by Stafford represents absolute faith and trust in God, His word, and His Kingdom to come. A positive from a tragedy---GOD'S SILVER LINING. Yes, all is well with my soul.

Something to think about.

P.S. For those who feel they cannot sing, just take 15-30 minutes quiet time, read the words, and reflect. One does not have to sing to enjoy God's message.

42. LIVE OR DIE.

The movie, "Cat on A Hot Tin Roof", features a confrontational scene between Burl Ives, (dying father) and Paul Newman (alcoholic and bitter son). During the scene involving many emotional exchanges, Ives stated, "I've got the guts to die, what I want to know is whether you have the guts to live?" Living in today's world is not an easy task.

Do you have the "guts" to live as a Christian/Jesus-follower? You must choose between the sacrificial and servant lifestyle of Jesus or the much easier, though more deadly, focus-on-personal-pleasures-lifestyle of Satan. Sounds ridiculous doesn't it? I mean, having to choose between Jesus and Satan! Who wouldn't choose Jesus?

Yet, GOD requires you to <u>live</u> the choice. James, the no-nonsense follower, stated it this way: "Don't you realize that friendship with the world makes you an enemy of GOD? I say it again: If you want to be a friend of the world, you make yourself an enemy of GOD. Do you think the Scriptures have no meaning? They say that GOD is passionate that <u>the spirit He has placed within us should be faithful to Him.</u>" James 4:4-5.

Be aware also, the devil does not come at you dressed in a red cape and pointed ears. He comes as <u>everything you've ever wished for.</u> (Tucker Max). Jesus comes asking you to give up the very things that Satan wants to give you.

Jesus said: "If any of you wants to be my follower, you must turn from your selfish ways, take up your cross, and follow me. If you try to hang onto your life, you will lose it. But of you give up your life for my sake and for the sake of the Good News, you will save it." Mark 8:34-35.

My dear reader, in your heart, you <u>know</u> the commitment and effort you are making to become a follower of Jesus. Most importantly, <u>God knows.</u> God gave you freedom of choice --- either you have the "guts" (actually love) to follow Jesus and "LIVE", or you choose the easier way of Satan and "DIE"!

People choosing their sinful nature are "easy pickins" for Satan. <u>It's You he's after!</u> The closer you get to Jesus, the more you distance yourself from Satan.

Something to think about.

P.S. Lao Tzu, Chinese philosopher, 6th century stated: "If you don't change direction, you may end up where you are headed.

43. THE HAPPINESS OF FORGIVENESS.

In the 1970's there was a television program named "Kung Fu", staring David Carradine as "Caine", a part Chinese man who fled from China because his "Master" had been killed. Caine wandered the West in search of his half-brother while assisting the helpless and avoiding Chinese bounty hunters.

In an episode entitled "Ancient Warrior" Caine met a man who was the sole survivor of a Native American tribe. That man had traveled back to land originally owned by his tribe so he could be buried there. His selected burial spot was under a tree, in the center of a small, pioneer town. A vote of the town council was needed to allow the burial. At the meeting, one councilman was strongly against this because a few years earlier members of the same Indian tribe, in a skirmish, killed his brother. When confronted with this bitterness, the Ancient Warrior told of an event several years prior to the "skirmish" wherein many members of his tribe, including women and children, were slaughtered by the town's people, and the land taken from the Native American tribe. He said to this man, "It is unfortunate that you have not learned the happiness of forgiveness."

"If you forgive those who sin against, your heavenly Father will forgive you. But if you refuse to forgive others, your heavenly Father will not forgive your sins." Matthew 6:14-15. This is clear and unambiguous.

<u>What is your happiness created by forgiveness?</u>

1. You become a "follower" of Jesus (see John 14:6).
2. You are spiritually "reborn" (see John 3:3).
3. Your salvation is assured when you belong to Christ Jesus (see Romans 8:1).
4. Your love grows more perfect living in GOD (see 1 John 4:17).
5. When you forgive, you are forgiven.

It isn't "time", rather it is "love" <u>that heals all wounds!</u> Experience the "happiness of forgiveness".

Something to think about.

44. PEER PRESSURE.

It has been defined as a feeling that one must do the same thing as other people of one's age or social group to be liked or respected by them. Most often this is associated with teenagers who unlawfully consume alcohol, take drugs, or engage in pre-marital sex because of the pressure from other teenagers.

If you think "peer pressure" is confined to teenagers, it is time for a reality check. Take some time, reflect, and conduct an inventory of your behavior after your teenage years. Did you experience hostility, quarreling, disrespect, envy, discrimination, selfish ambition, drunkenness, wild parties, unlawful acts, or other instances not spiritually motivated? Did friends or the customs of our surrounding world influence you in any way? Did you find comfort in having others behave believe in the same way? Did their behavior make it easier for you to do likewise? Did your behavior make it easier for them? Did athletic or other activities take precedence over attending church or related activities?

GOD gave you a brain and freedom of choice. Peer pressure is allowing someone else to do your thinking! The Scriptures provide you with GOD's answer to "peer pressure" and all earthly temptations, trials, and tribulations. "Don't copy the behavior and customs of this world, but let GOD transform you into a new person by changing the way you think." Romans 12:2. GOD is telling you to do your own thinking. If you believe and accept that Jesus is the "way, the truth, and the life" (see John 14:6), then peer pressure no longer exists. Do not let anyone or anything negatively affect your relationship with GOD

As parents, if you learn that your child has done something foolish and claims influence or pressure by a peer, your response might be: "I suppose if Dan jumped off a cliff, you would too!"

JESUS: "If others ignore Me as being The Way, The Truth, and The Life, will you also?"

Something to think about.

P.S. "Peer pressure" doesn't have to be negative. Surround yourself with "believers" and "followers" of Jesus, and joyfully live "the *real* way, the truth, and the life.

45. If I Were A Rich Man.....

Fortune 500 magazine ranks the richest people in the world as well as the largest United States corporations by total revenue. The magazine is consistent with man's infatuation with wealth and other earthly desires.

As Jesus was starting out on His way to Jerusalem, a rich man came running up to Him, knelt down and asked Jesus what he must do to inherit eternal life. After a short discussion Jesus told the man to sell all his possessions, give the money to the poor, (he will have treasures in heaven) and then come follow Him. The man went away sad, for he had many possessions (see Mark 10:17-21).

"Teach those who are <u>rich in this world</u> not to be proud and not to trust in their money, which is so unreliable. Their trust should be in God who richly <u>gives us all</u> we need for our enjoyment. Tell them to use their money to do good works and be generous to those in need, always be willing to share with others. By doing this they will be storing up their treasure as a good foundation for the future so that they may experience <u>true life.</u>"
1 Timothy 6:17-19.

Thought #1: Re-read the above from Paul's letter to Timothy and ask yourself whether you are <u>sharing</u> your wealth as well as the "richness" of the "spiritual gifts" God has given you. A spiritual gift is given to each of us so we can <u>help each other.</u>" (see 1 Corinthians 12:7).

These gifts can be of speech, to teach, to heal, to lead, to administer, to cleanup, be generally helpful, or other gifts. All gifts are equally valued and equally needed in the world (see 1 Corinthians, Chapter 12). If you feel you could/should be doing more, let's start now.

Thought #2: Have you ever thought negatively about people who have large amounts of money, i.e., they must have exploited others, committed unlawful acts, were deceitful and conniving, had selfish ambition, or were greedy? Jesus said you do not sit in judgment of others (see Luke 6:17). Jesus will decide whether the rich possess their possessions, or their possessions possess them. Your relationship is between you and GOD. Give *that* your full attention.

In your heart, you already know that true "richness" is the next world.

Something to think about.

46. God's View: Two Words and One Man.

Upon reflection, I believe we are the happiest when we serve or assist others and make them happy. So, "let's be the happiest we can be!"

FACTS: I grew up in South Dakota where the winters were never mild and often brutal. In the mid 1950s, after a nice, 16 inches of new snow, it would pile up on the streets. At that time the snow plows were few and far between, and neither the motor vehicles nor their tires were sufficiently advanced to address the road conditions. When I was about 13-15 years of age, a friend and I would walk around the neighborhoods and the downtown area and help people either dig out of the snowbanks or help push them when they were stuck in the accumulated snow. I vividly remember people being so happy to receive the assistance. They would be smiling at us, and so often, as they "zig-zagged" through the snow away from us, they would stick their arm out of the window and wave. Yup, just one hand on the "no-power-steering" steering wheel, but they had to express their thanks for the help.

No money was given, and none was expected. A "thank you" or "bless you" was *more* than sufficient. The feeling we had was euphoric. The happiness on other people's faces was not only satisfying, but we knew that they would reciprocate if the situation presented itself. We set an example. We were working together in harmony. And we couldn't help but think, "Gad, this is really fun!" I just know GOD was smiling (and perhaps thinking maybe He should send more snow!).

ISSUE: How does this exemplify GOD's view of the world?

"Above all, clothe yourselves with <u>love,</u> which binds all of us together in <u>perfect</u> <u>harmony.</u>" Colossians 3:14. Jesus: "For even the Son of Man came not to be served but to serve others and to give his life as a ransom for many." Matthew 20:28.

GOD's two words: Love & Serve.

GOD's one man: Jesus Christ. John 3:16: "For this is how GOD loved the world..."

Something to think about.

47. PERSONALIZING LIFE'S JOURNEY. (TAKE IT PERSONALLY)

During my tenure as a circuit court judge, I have seen human behavior at its worst, i.e. murder, aggravated assaults, rape, molestations, thievery, lying, cheating, addictions, greed, envy, neglect or abuse of children. But I have also seen the absolute amazement of undying and unrelenting love in action. I witnessed men who suffered from alcohol addiction day-in and day-out and the wives who would not give up on them. Whether it involved helping them home from a bar or sitting next to them in church while they were inebriated, these ladies held steadfastly. They had an option; they could have "thrown in the towel", but they did not. I am convinced that it was not the legal commitment, rather their ability to love unconditionally. Their love was "personal" --- and so is GOD's!

You have heard, "Now, don't take this personally, but" --- - forget about that and take GOD's message "personally" because that is how He intends it. St. Augustine was quoted as saying, "GOD loves each of us as if there were only one of us." Few have said it better.

The next time you are reflecting on your own personal journey and its ramifications, think "GOD AND ME" and be assured:

- GOD knew ME before I was born, and had a plan of salvation for ME (see Jeremiah 1:5 & 29:11; Ephesians 1:4-5).
- GOD loves ME unconditionally and always (see Romans 8:31-39).
- Jesus died for ME (see Galatians 2:20).
- Jesus rose from the dead for ME (see Matthew 28:5-10).
- Jesus gives eternal life to Me (see John 10:27-28).
- GOD sees ME as equal to all others (see Romans 2:11; Proverbs 22:2).
- GOD does not test ME beyond MY strength; shows ME a way out (see 1 Cor. 10:13).
- GOD forgives and forgets the sins of ME (see Hebrews 8:12).
- GOD warned ME about the devil (see 1 Peter 5:8-9).
- On judgment day, Jesus is an advocate for ME (see 1 John 2:1).
- GOD's Kingdom awaits ME (see Matthew 7:21).

Take it personally! GOD does.

Something to think about.

48. Recognizing God's Hints.

A "hint" is defined as: understand, accept, or act upon a message or direction that has been communicated indirectly.

Indulge me for a short time. A few months ago, in grocery store in Sun City West, Arizona, I was standing in a "15 items or less" line. There was a lady in front of me with her groceries being processed. As I was standing there, a thought entered my head, "what if this lady could not pay for her groceries, would I pay for them?" I told myself I would. When the cashier totaled her groceries, the lady reached into each pocket and purse looking for her credit card. The longer it took, the more frantic she became. I finally asked her, "Ma'am, let me pay for your groceries." She declined and continued searching for her card. She had just gotten gas, so she asked the cashier to call the station in case she dropped it there. No such luck. Again, I said, "Ma'am, please let me pay for your groceries." She reluctantly agreed and thanked me several times. She left, and after purchasing my groceries, I left.

She saw me crossing the parking lot and called me over to her vehicle. As I stood there, she opened her car door. There, laying on the front seat, was her wallet with her credit card inside. She was so happy and wanted to go back into the store and get me paid. We had a short visit while I insisted that it was not necessary, that the good Lord wanted us to meet and He chose this manner. She, again, asked my name and said, "I am going to tell my church members about you and prayers will be said." The thought of having a whole church praying for me far exceeded the dollars spent!

You can interpret this story as you want, but I fervently believe this experience was a "hint" from GOD. I don't mean to imply that I have a "higher connection" with the Lord, because I don't. I invite you to reflect on your life -- were there certain times when you felt a "hint or nudge" to serve your fellow man? If so, don't be amazed. "For GOD is working in you, giving you the desire and the power to do what pleases him." Philippians 2:13.

When you receive a nudge, hint, or whisper from GOD, don't ignore it.

Something to think about.

49. THE LITTLE ENGINE THAT COULD.

"The Little Engine That Could" is a fairytale (circa 1930), designed to teach children the value of optimism, persistence, and hard work. The story, summarized, is about a train engine refusing to pull its many cars over a long, steep mountain after the original engine breaks down and is unable to perform the task. Other, larger engines decline <u>feeling it is too difficult.</u> Finally, the "little engine" was asked, and agreed to try. As the Little Engine approached the peak of the mountain, it kept chugging hard saying, "I think I can, I think I can, I think I can." And due to hard work, persistence, and believing in itself, the Little Engine reached the mountain top and headed down the grade on the other side, saying, "I thought I could, I thought I could, I thought I could!"

And how is your engine? Have you, when confronted with life's problems, ever wondered if you can successfully address them? Scripture tells you that when you persevere and conquer, you gain character and confidence, with the reward being the Kingdom of Heaven (see Romans 5:3-4; James 1:2-4; 1 Peter 1:6). We take tests in school, to determine if we pass and, often, to determine if we qualify to administer to public demands and needs. How do we NOT expect to be tested in life to determine our acceptance to GOD? This is not an <u>"all-nighter"</u> before an exam; this is an <u>"all-lifer"</u> on a daily basis --- before *the* "final" exam!

Life's trials are not easy, but you are not in this alone. Scripture reveals that you are precious to GOD, and He is always available to ease your burdens and provide you with an abundance of grace for your journey --- all for the asking. If gasoline were free, would you hesitate to ask for some? Free gas in your car's tank will take you only so far, but GOD's free gifts will take you all the way to Jesus who is patiently waiting for you.

Please don't ignore this story because it was a learning device for children. We must become like little children to enter the kingdom (see Matthew 18:3). The outcome for the Little Engine was uncertain. If you accept Jesus into your life you are given a new life and your outcome *is* assured. (see Galatians 2:20). "The reward for trusting him will be the salvation of our souls." 1 Peter 1:9.

And Jesus just said, "I knew you could, I knew you could, I knew you could!"

Something to think about.

Keep chugging!

50. SCARED THE DEVIL OUT OF ME.

It is an expression sometimes used when one is frightened far beyond normal. "You scared the devil out of me!"

We all struggle with sinning and, as I see it, there are three aspects of sin in our lives: (1) Personal sinful nature: "I have discovered this principle of life---that when I want to do what is right, I inevitably do what is wrong. I love God's law with all my heart. But there is another power within me that is at war with my mind. This power makes me a slave to the sin that is still within me." Romans 7:21-23. (2) Influence of the world: "Don't copy the behavior and customs of this world, but let God transform you into a new person by changing the way you think. Then you will learn to know God's will for you, which is good and pleasing." Romans 12:2. (3) The devil himself: we find the serpent deceitfully tempting Eve in Genesis chapter 3; in John 13:2 at the last supper, the devil had already prompted Judas to betray Jesus. Satan has blinded the minds of those who don't believe (see Ephesians 6:11); we are to stand firm against all strategies of the devil; and 1 Peter 5:8-9 tells us to stay alert and watch for your *great enemy* the devil."

Be strong against the devil and be strong in your faith. Listen up: the devil is an *enemy* of God and destined for hell. The devil is among us and he never met a soul he didn't WANT. The devil even tempted Jesus (see Matthew 4:1-11) I am not being judgmental -- the purpose of this discussion is to allow you to reflect, and determine if you are ignoring God and making way for the devil in your life. "Dear children, don't let anyone deceive you about this: When people do what is right, it shows they are righteous, even as Christ is righteous. But when people keep on sinning, it shows that they belong to the devil, who has been sinning since the beginning. But the Son of God came to destroy the works of the devil. Those who have been born into God's family do not make a practice of sinning, because God's life is in them. So, they can't keep on sinning, because they are children of God." 1 John 3:7-9. "Oh, what a miserable person I am. Who will free me from this life that is dominated by sin and death? Thank God! The answer is in Jesus Christ our Lord." Romans 7:24-25.

Receive Jesus. "Scare" out the devil, and let the loving presence of Jesus make you a "*child* of God", not an enemy.

If only I had known, I would have done this years ago. Well, now *you* know, too.

Something to think about.

51. STOP, LOOK, AND LISTEN.

Requests or demands "to listen" are made on us every day, i.e. parents, government, teachers, salespeople, ministers, politicians, etc. They want us to stop what we are doing, look at them, and listen. GOD wants us to do the same and learn about LOVE.

GOD wants you to remember His <u>inseparable love for you;</u> but also learn His expectation of love <u>from you;</u> *and* learn His expectation of <u>your love for one another.</u>

Jesus: "You must love the Lord your GOD with all your heart, all your soul, and all your mind. This is the <u>first AND greatest commandment.</u>" Matthew 22:37-38.

Jesus: "<u>A second is equally important:</u> Love your neighbor as yourself." Matthew 22:39. Our love for others should model Christ's love for us (see Ephesians 5:2).

And, what about the neighbors you don't get along with?

Jesus: "<u>But to those who are WILLING TO LISTEN,</u> I say love your enemies! Do good to those who hate you. Bless those who curse you. Pray for those who hurt you." Luke 6:27-29. "In this way you will be acting as true children of your Father in heaven. For he gives his sunlight to both the evil and the good and he sends rain on the just and the unjust alike." Matthew 5:43-45. If you find it difficult to love a particular person, please remember, Jesus does not!

Soul Alert: STOP, LOOK, LISTEN: Stop what you are doing ---- Look at the Scriptures ---- Be willing to listen to Jesus and practice love.

Time Alert: "How do you know what your life will be like tomorrow? Your life is like the morning fog --- it is here a little while, then it's gone." James 4:14.

Don't be arrogant and foolish enough to think "there is always time"! Your morning fog --- here a little while, and then gone.

Don't think about it---------DO!

52. This Is For All The Marbles.

Facts: A final putt in a golf tournament, a last pitch in the final World Series game, a last free-throw, or a last kicked field goal opportunity --- all to determine the victor. Sometimes the broadcaster will say, "this is for all the marbles!"

Question: Can you identify with and really fathom "all the marbles" spiritually?

"No eye has seen, no ear has heard, and no mind has imagined what God has prepared for those who love him." 1 Corinthians 2:9. "When we tell you these things, we do not use words that come from human wisdom. Instead, we speak words given to us by the Spirit, using the Spirit's words to explain spiritual truths." 1 Corinthians 2:13. Our human brain cannot fathom this gift from God.

Saint Maria Faustina Kowalska, was born in Poland in 1905 and joined the Congregation of Sisters of Our Lady of Mercy. Over several years, she wrote a diary she said was based on her conversations with Jesus Christ. In this diary she relates her opportunity to visit hell which she describes as follows: "It is a place of great torture; how awesomely large and extensive it is! The kinds of torture I saw: first, the torture that constitutes hell is the loss of God; second, the perpetual remorse of conscience; third is that one's condition will never change; fourth is the fire that will penetrate the soul without destroying it---a terrible suffering, since it is a purely spiritual fire, lit by God's anger; <u>fifth</u> is the continual darkness and a terrible, suffocating smell, and despite the darkness, the devils and the souls of the damned see each other and all the evil, both of others and their own; <u>sixth</u> is the constant company of Satan; <u>seventh</u> is the horrible despair, hatred of God, vile words, curses and blasphemies." *

Among all of this suffering, Sister Kowalska noticed that <u>most of the souls there are those who DISBELIEVED that there was a hell.</u> Whether you believe Sister Kowalska's account or not, <u>don't disbelieve there is a hell.</u> Revelation 21:8.

Heaven or hell --- Your choice "<u>for all the marbles</u>"!

Something to really think about.

*Diary of Saint Maria Faustina Kowalska Notebook II, #741 at page 296-7. Marian Press, Stockbridge, Maine.

53. I WANT YOUR WILL TO BE DONE, NOT MINE.

"There is one GOD, the Father, by whom all things were created, and <u>for</u> whom we live. And there is one Lord, Jesus Christ, through whom all things were created, and <u>through</u> whom we live." 1 Corinthians 8:6. So, <u>we live for GOD, and through Christ.</u> When sent to earth, Jesus gave up his divine privileges and was born as a human being. (see Philippians 2:7). "This high priest (Jesus) of ours understands our weaknesses, for He faced all of the same testing we did, yet He did not sin." Hebrews 4:15.

Question: How did Jesus not succumb to his sinful nature and how did He maintain His control through the Holy Spirit? I suggest the following.

1. Jesus used the "Word" as a weapon against Satan when tempted, i.e. Jesus said, "The Scriptures say .... (see Matthew 4:1-11). The "Word of GOD" is an offensive weapon you can use against Satan (see Ephesians 6:17).

2. <u>"Yet I want your will to be done, not mine."</u> Luke 22:42; Mark 14:36. Jesus was always aware of the Father's plan for him. Jesus did not "pass the cup" but stayed on course and persevered to his death. <u>We can use the commitment of Jesus for our journey to salvation.</u>

3. Constant guidance and control from the Holy Spirit---thinking of only things that please the

Spirit (see Romans 8:5). The Holy Spirit produces love, joy, peace, patience, and self-control (see Galatians 5:22-23).

Listen up: <u>Right now, you have the same knowledge and help that Jesus had!</u> You can utilize the same strategy that Jesus used to defeat the sinful nature of man and persevere in accordance with the Father's plan for your salvation. Further, the Holy Spirit will teach you everything you need and <u>remind you</u> of everything Jesus has told you (see John 14:26).

And since you live <u>after</u> Jesus' Resurrection you have living and written <u>proof</u> of eternal life after death.

You can do this!

Something to think about.

54. HELP NEEDED OR JUST PLAIN LAZY.

In lieu of a national tragedy, it is not difficult to determine those who "need" help. These are the poor and physically or mentally affected who cannot function at a job; those unable to help themselves. We already know from Scripture, that all of us are part of the Body of Christ, and therefore obligated to work for the good of all and assist our fellow-man. No one person is more valuable than another, and we all need each other (see 1 Corinthians Chapter 12).

What does Scripture say about those who don't qualify as "help-needed"? In 2 Thessalonians 3:6-15, Paul gave these commands:

1. Stay away from all believers who live idle lives and don't follow the tradition of working hard day and night, so as not to be a burden to anyone. Those unwilling to work will not get to eat.
2. Those living idle lives, refusing to work and meddling in other people's business, are urged in the name of the Lord Jesus Christ to settle down and work to earn their own living.
3. Stay away from those who refuse to obey this (Paul's) letter, so they will be ashamed. Don't think of them as enemies but warn them as you would a brother or sister.

4. For the rest of the dear brothers and sisters, never get tired of doing good.

We always seem to come back to how we want to live as opposed to how GOD wants us to responsively live. This may very well be a reason why many refuse to read scripture.

This notwithstanding, I believe this letter of Paul (don't be lazy and help others) changes the John F. Kennedy inaugural quote of 1961, in this fashion:

AND SO, MY FELLOW AMERICANS, ASK NOT WHAT YOUR FELLOW MAN CAN DO FOR YOU, ASK WHAT YOU CAN DO FOR YOUR FELLOW MAN!

Something to think about.

55. NEVER GIVE UP.

"Many of life's failures are experienced by people who did not realize how close they were to success when they gave up." (Thomas Edison.)

"So, let us never get tired of doing what is good. At just the right time we will reap a harvest of blessings <u>if we don't give up.</u>" Galatians 6:9. Scripture further tells us that even though our bodies are dying, Jesus is renewing our spirits each day. And, He assures us that our present troubles are small and won't last very long. They produce for us a glory that vastly outweighs our problems and will last forever (see 2 Corinthians 4:16-18).

Disappointment, frustration, loneliness, anxiety, personal losses, can all render life discouraging, debilitating, and defeating. Sometimes you need more than an additional Bible verse to sustain your momentum. Let me suggest the following "booster rocket" for continuing your life journey to Jesus:

1. Jesus lived as "man", fully experiencing all human struggles.
2. Jesus did <u>not quit</u>; He persevered and did what the Father wanted, earning for you total forgiveness of your sins, eternal life, and heaven.
3. Jesus will NEVER give up on you!
4. Jesus is patiently waiting for you.

<u>Jesus does all of this for YOU, so you don't give up.</u>

Have you ever thought or said, "I won't stop, even if it <u>kills me!</u> "If you try to hang on to your life, you will lose it. But if you <u>give up your life for my sake,</u> you will save it." Matthew 16:25.

Jesus continues to be the "Something to think about."

56. JUDGMENT.

I served for twenty-three years as a judge presiding over a large variety of legal actions between mankind. I had authorization from the State to handle most kinds of cases -- and the *obligation* to do it fairly. I am but a man in a job of the world. But, the LORD is the one who judges us spiritually.

"Do not judge others, and you will not be judged. For you will be treated as you treat others. The standard you use in judging is the standard by which you will be judged." Matthew 7:1-3

"So don't make judgments about anyone ahead of time -- before the Lord returns. For he will bring our darkest secrets to light and will reveal our private motives. Then GOD will give to each one whatever praise is due." 1 Corinthians 4:5. We cannot know the thoughts and feelings of others -- why they did what they did. Those without the facts should remain silent. Focus on YOUR conduct, not someone else's.

"You must give an account on judgment day for every idle word you speak. The words you say will either acquit you or condemn you." Matthew 12:36. Focus on YOUR words and not someone else's.

"Yes, each of us will give a personal account to GOD. So let's stop condemning each other. <u>Decide instead to live</u>

in such a way that you will not cause another believer to stumble and fall." Romans 14:12-13.

Judgment for you and all mankind comes when the Lord returns. Spend your time preparing for the "return" of Jesus. Pray incessantly.

Something to remember to think about.

57. NEVER RELINQUISH THE PROGRESS MADE.

For the past years I, along with a recovering alcoholic friend, meet and talk with men in a group rehabilitation center in the Phoenix area. These individuals consist of street people, some with addiction problems, some recently paroled, and some simply overwhelmed with life's problems. The chances of these people stumbling or falling back into old habits is great.

Paul taught with Scriptures that one should forget the past and look forward to the future -- the heavenly prize for which GOD, through Christ Jesus, is calling us. However, Paul recognized that many with addictions or heavy burdens will suffer relapses, that all of us are not perfect, so we also may stumble along the way. <u>"But we must hold on to the progress we have already made."</u> Philippians 3:16.

<u>A stumble does not eliminate prior progress.</u> It is not a "start-over". Pick up where you left off, pray, and ask GOD for assistance. None of us are immune from burdens and back-slides. This is precisely why Jesus invites you to come to Him with your weariness and burdens and find rest for your soul.

"My grace is all you need. <u>My power works best in weakness.</u> So now <u>I am glad to boast about my</u>

weaknesses, so that the power of Christ can work through me." 2 Corinthians 12:9.

Asking Jesus for help is not a sign of weakness or being ashamed, but rather a recognition that we cannot survive our spiritual journey alone.

Something to think about.

58. Searching For The Truth.

The legal profession has often been described as a "search for the truth". As a circuit judge I had many opportunities to witness, as well as conduct, the "search" for the truth. Justice in this world requires the finding of true facts. This is an inherent problem because the facts are often contested, and the determination of the true facts is for the judge or the jury, i.e. "The light was red", "the light was green"; "I told him this", "no he did not" (nothing in writing). In God's world there is no search since God knows everything. Can you imagine a proceeding without ever having to swear in a witness?!

But this predicament is not restricted to the legal profession. Your whole life can be a "search". You see decisions and statements being made every day, in all facets of life, where you find truth lacking. Bearing false witness causes mistrust, disappointment, disgust, anger, lack of confidence, unfairness, and negative thoughts.

Although <u>the truth is not a guarantee in this world, IT IS AVAILABLE!</u>

Jesus tells you that He is the <u>truth</u> (see John 14:6); if you remain faithful to me, you will "know the truth and the truth will set you free." John 8:31-32. "Free" means that because you belong to Him, Jesus has freed you from the power of sin that leads to death (see Romans 8:2).

When the Father sent his only Son, "the Truth", to die for our sins, and then raised Jesus from the dead, the spiritual "search for the truth" was over! This "truth" has been available to each of us for over 2000 years.

Start now and be ready when the "Truth" returns to earth to get YOU!

Something to think about.

59. A MOMENT OF RIGHTEOUSNESS.

I went into a grocery store in Sun City West, Arizona to purchase some groceries. Picking up about five items, I was standing in line for check-out. My grocery items got inter-mingled with the lady's ahead of me and the clerk made a sarcastic remark, which I questioned, and we had words. I put my items back into the basket, returned them to the shelf and left the store. After a few days of hoping I could avoid this clerk, I thought "this is really stupid" especially if I thought I was a "follower" of Jesus. So, I approached this clerk, reminded her of our verbal exchange, and apologized for what I had said. She also apologized. When I left the store and when taking the receipt from her, <u>she grabbed my hand with both of her hands, and said, "thank you."</u> It was a mutual happiness of forgiveness.

A story was told to me about a mother and eight-year-old daughter who had gone through a drive-up at a fast food restaurant. On the way home the daughter discovered that they received an extra order of food and suggested they should return the food. The mother had a busy schedule, and was under some pressure, but did go back and return the food. Afterward, on the way home, the daughter said, "Do you hear that music mom?" Mom said, "what music?" The daughter said, "<u>the singing in my heart!</u>"

During our lifetime there are instances when we do just what GOD wants. Through the negatives of life, the complaints, the pressures, the lies, the frustrations, and our sinful acts, our behavior can still epitomize the teachings of Jesus. It is a "living like Jesus" feeling which brings with it comfort, warmth, happiness, satisfaction, confidence, acceptance, and an extraordinary feeling of closeness to Jesus. "I become righteous through faith in Christ." Philippians 3:9.

I call this a "moment of righteousness". When our thoughts are heavenly; earthly concerns are gone; our heart is near-bursting; we savor the feeling, and realize that we, although for only a moment, have indeed put a smile on the face of GOD.

Let's make GOD smile again and again.

Something to think about.

60. Absorbing the Depth of the Death and Resurrection of Jesus.

Jesus' death took away your sins and His resurrection gives you eternal life, where GOD will wipe away every tear from your eyes, and there will be no more death or sorrow or crying or pain. All these things are gone forever (see Romans 4:25; Revelation 20:4). Have you ever taken the time to completely <u>absorb</u> the full meaning of <u>each of the above events</u>? If yes, then you experienced an ultimate closeness with Jesus. If not, then let's pursue it.

1. "For GOD presented Jesus as the sacrifice for our (yours and mine) sins. People are made right with GOD when they believe that Jesus sacrificed his life, shedding his blood." Romans 3:25.

2. The resurrection of Jesus is a historical fact. (see Matthew 28:5-10). "And if Christ had not been raised, then your faith is worthless, and you are still guilty of your sins." 1 Corinthians 15:17. "But in fact, Christ did rise from the dead." 1 Corinthians 15:20. And if you openly declare that Jesus is Lord and believe that GOD raised him from the dead, then you will be saved (see Romans 10:9-10).

Undoubtedly these are the two most pivotal circumstances in the history of mankind and for over 2000 years man has been given the opportunity, through Scripture and Holy Spirit, to fully understand GOD's love. Jesus' death took away your sins; His resurrection gives you eternal life. Absorb it; feel it!

When I absorb and feel the depth of the death and resurrection, my soul hears the Carpenter duo's song: *"There's a Kind of Hush"*, as amended:

There's a kind of hush, all over the world,
All over the world you can feel Jesus' love;
Absorb and feel with me now----you will see what I mean--
--It isn't a dream,
The only sound that you will hear, is when JESUS whispers in your ear;
I LOVE YOU----FOR EVER AND EVER.

Absorb the depth of following Christ; feel the "hush"; be eternally grateful.

Something to think about.

61. THE DIRECTNESS OF JESUS.

One of my loves from childhood through adulthood is watching western movies. Yes, the "good guy" prevails, and the "bad guy" ends up in jail! The demeanor of the cowboy has changed over the years, but nonetheless I appreciate the good cowboy as an enforcer of justice for those acting outside the law. During Jesus' time here on earth some people "needed a good tongue lashing", or other "corrective action", when they traveled outside GOD's law. Jesus obliged.

1. <u>Paul, once known as Saul</u>: A murderer of Christians, was knocked off his horse by GOD on the way to Damascus and was converted to Christianity (see Acts 9:1-19). The people watched a confirmed Christian killer converted into a confirmed Christian supporter and effective leader!

2. <u>Peter:</u> "Get behind me, Satan," spoken to Peter by Jesus. "You are seeing things merely from a human point of view, not from GOD's." Mark 8:33. The background is that Jesus was telling His disciples about His upcoming arrest, suffering, and death. Peter tried to reprimand Jesus for saying such things. Peter's actions were contrary to the Father's plan, consistent with earthly desires, and the thoughts of Satan. So, Jesus said Get.........!

3. <u>Teachers & Pharisees:</u> "But I warn you---unless your righteousness is better than the righteousness of the teachers of religious law and the Pharisees, you will never enter the Kingdom of Heaven!" Matthew 5:20. "For they don't practice what they teach. They crush people with unbearable religious demands and never lift a finger to ease the burden." Matthew 23:3-4. Sorrow awaits the teachers of religious law and Pharisees ---- Hypocrites!" (see Matthew 23:23-33).

4. <u>Money changers and merchants in the Temple area:</u> Jesus drove them out with anger and a whip (see John 2:14-16).

"For we must all stand before Jesus to be judged. We will each receive whatever we deserve for the good or evil we have done in this earthly body." 2 Corinthians 5:10 -- the ultimate "directness" of Jesus.

Something to think about.

62. SOUL WINNER.

When Jesus first met disciples Simon (Peter), James, Andrew, and John He said to them "Come follow me, and I will show you how to fish for people." Matthew 4:19, Luke 5:1-11. Simon (Peter), after Jesus' resurrection, was asked three times if he loved Jesus, and each time Peter responded, "You know I love you." Jesus said, "Then feed my sheep." John 21:15-17.

The message of Jesus to each of us is all about loving, helping, serving, forgiving and inspiring others. Read the book inspired by GOD (Bible). Crave its spiritual milk. Grow into a full experience of salvation (see 1 Peter 2:2). Receive and believe in Jesus as your Savior and the only way to salvation. Your life with Jesus provides peace, forgiveness, assurance of salvation, *and* the obligation to share your faith. Jesus said to His disciples: "Go into all the world and preach the Good News (about Jesus the Messiah, His death, resurrection, and gift of eternal life) to everyone." Mark 16:15.

A "Soul Winner" is one who actively shares his or her faith with others in order to lead them to Christ * -- also called "Laborers" (see Matthew 9:37-38).

"But my life is worth nothing to me unless I use it for finishing the work assigned me by the Lord Jesus – the work of telling others the Good News about the wonderful grace of GOD." Acts 20:24.

"There is more joy in heaven over one lost sinner who repents and returns to God than over ninety-nine others who are righteous and haven't strayed away." Luke 15:7.

"He said to his disciples, 'The harvest is great, but the workers are few. So, pray to the Lord who is in charge of the harvest; <u>ask Him to send more workers into His fields.</u>'" Matthew 9:37-38.

Be a laborer, a "Soul Winner" -- a fisher of men and women -- Give heaven "joy" time and time again!

Something to think about.

Personal note from the Author: My wife, Sandra, has, for years, been active in Stonecroft Ministries, Christian Women's Connection and Bible study (see Stonecroft.org). I have watched her pray and anguish over her desire to see more people brought to Jesus. She would remark: "There are just so many out there who don't KNOW Jesus." She has been a "soul winner" long before I understood and discovered the term existed. I now comprehend her thoughts <u>and the thoughts of others like her</u>, her anguish, her disappointment, her hope, her prayers...for, as she likes to say, "the not-yet-saved". She, again, has taught me about learning to be a disciple of Jesus, and to have the confidence to be a "soul winner" myself. I thank her for that now, and I'm sure I will again.

* from "New Believer's Bible" Glossary, page-382.

63. ALL FOR ONE, ONE FOR ALL.

Jesus said this long before the "The Three Musketeers"!

All for one means <u>no one</u> is left behind. Consider the Lost Sheep Parable — a man has 100 sheep and loses one; he will leave the 99 and search for the lost one. "There is more joy in heaven over one lost sinner who repents and returns to God than over ninety-nine others who are righteous and haven't strayed away." Luke 15:3-7.

One for all means each person contributes to the whole. In July, 1969 our country landed a man on the moon. NASA estimated that more than 400,000 engineers, scientists, technicians, and other personnel worked over the years to accomplish the several moon landings. For these landings to be successful, all had to perform their skill — and in cooperation with each other. It was a team effort.

"A spiritual gift is given to each of us so we can help each other." 1 Corinthians 12:7. There are different kinds of spiritual gifts (different abilities); no gift of the Holy Spirit is "better" than another (no person more valuable); every single person has a vital role to play and we need each other to function as God intended. This includes all individuals, Jews, gentiles, slaves, or free. When we believe Jesus is our Savior, we are all baptized into one body by the Holy Spirit. All of us together are Christ's body – working in harmony. GOD also planned a "team effort" (see 1 Corinthians Chapter 12).

On GOD's team you develop a "love", not the kind of love for your spouse, but the kind of love for your fellow man, as Jesus taught. This love commits you to taking care of the thirsty, the hungry, the naked, the homeless, the imprisoned, the sick, and bury the dead (see Matthew 25:35-40).

Jesus is the "One for All". You/we are the "All for One"!

Something to think about.

P.S. "If you think you are too important to help someone, you are only fooling yourself. You are not that important." Galatians 6:3.

Something more to think about!

64. GOD'S SPIRITUAL HOME RUN FROM FRANCIS OF ASSISI.

Francis of Assisi was born in Italy in 1182 and died in 1226. During his short lifetime he founded a religious order called the Franciscans. Francis was renowned for his love, simplicity, and practice of poverty. He spent his vast wealth serving the needs of the poor. He was seen as living like Jesus.

Francis of Assisi once stated: "Start by doing what's necessary; then do what is possible; and suddenly you are doing the impossible."

NECESSARY: Love the Lord your GOD with all your heart, mind, and soul. Love your neighbor as yourself, even those who hurt, persecute, hate, and curse you (see Matthew 22:37-39; Luke 6:27-36).

POSSIBLE: Forgive and forget (see Hebrews 8:12). GOD has <u>done this</u> and <u>continues</u> to do so. Jesus did this as a human being. So can you if you have accepted Jesus and He lives in you.

SUDDENLY WE ARE DOING THE IMPOSSIBLE: Thy Kingdom come, <u>Thy will be done on earth as it is in heaven.</u> (Lord's prayer, see Matthew 6:5-15). Can you imagine doing GOD's will on earth as it is in heaven? Yes, doing the impossible. Could this conceivably mean that the world would no longer be ruled by Satan? <u>Now *that's* a home run!</u>

Jesus guided us in prayer to GOD the Father. Matthew 6:5-15. And I don't believe He was just moving the air around! Has your reciting of the Lord's prayer become just a *robotic movement of your lips?* Do you dare admit, <u>"Forgive me, Father, for I know not what I've been saying?"</u>

The bottom line comes from James 1:22 "But, don't just listen to GOD's word, you must <u>do</u> what it says. Otherwise, you are only fooling yourselves."

Something to think about.

P.S. The observation of Francis' convictions is not confined to the Thirteenth Century! Through GOD's Word and the teachings of Jesus, we know GOD's will for us. GOD created man. Man created evil, sufferings, and selfishness. Doing GOD's will has always been, and continues to be, the solution -- and the "home run" of Francis, you, and others.

65. War with Hell.

Being spiritually "reborn," is professing the love of GOD, the life of Jesus, and GOD's plan of salvation for us. However, it would be remiss to not emphasize the existence of hell and the war inherent therein. Make no mistake, <u>your life is a war between Satan and your eternal soul. It is daily, and it is constant!</u> Satan is destined for hell --- FOREVER. Are you going to <u>choose</u> to go with Satan?

Satan is not a fellow human, but a fallen angel, the great deceiver, a spiritual host of this wicked world (see Ephesians 6:12-13). Do not underestimate Satan and don't be lulled into believing that there is no war, no urgency, or that hell is only for the "really bad people", or even worse, believing there is no hell. Remember, <u>SATAN NEVER MET A SOUL HE DIDN'T WANT!</u> He even boldly tried taking the soul of Jesus! (see Matthew 4: 1-11).

If you suffer from the desires of your sinful nature, i.e., sexual immorality, lustful pleasures, hostility, quarreling, jealousy, outbursts of anger, division, wild parties, selfish ambition, envy, greed, pride in achievements and possessions, and a general craving for everything you see, then <u>Satan is winning his war with you and you will not inherit the Kingdom of GOD</u> (see Galatians 5:19).

The Bible is comprehensive when enumerating the horrors of hell. You have no excuse of being uninformed, neither to hell's existence nor its consequences (see 2 Thessalonians 1:8-9, Revelation 20:10, Luke 16:19-26).

Today, you are not irreparably separated from GOD; you have access to protection from the devil and all his demons; you are free from torment day and night; free of unquenchable fire; and -- you still have your freedom of choice between heaven and hell.

Catch this: in hell you *are separated* from GOD's presence; you live with the devil and all of hell's sufferings, and lose your freedom of choice -- *forever.*

We have discussed long enough the existence and horrors of hell and going there; let's, in this life, concentrate instead on *avoiding hell.*

"So we will not be afraid on the day of judgement, we will face Him with confidence because we live like Jesus here in this world." 1 John 4:17. "But the Lord is faithful; He will strengthen you and guard you from the evil one." 2 Thessalonians 3:3.

Live with the devil? Now that ought to "scare the you know what out of you!"

Something to think about.

Please pray, and accept the unconditional love of GOD!

66. JESUS, THE GREATEST WITNESS EVER.

As a long-time trial judge, I have seen lawyers relentlessly question witnesses in an effort to affect the truthfulness and believability of that witness. Similarly, Pharisees in Jesus' time mercilessly questioned Jesus with similar intent to discredit His testimony both for Mankind and for His Father:

JESUS, testifying as the WITNESS FOR MANKIND:
("P" = Pharisees. "J" = Jesus.)

P: "Now tell us---is it right to pay taxes to Caesar or not?"
J: "Why are trying to trap me? Show me a Roman coin, and I'll tell you. Whose picture and title are stamped on it?
P: "Caesar's," they replied."
J: "Well then, give to Caesar what belongs to Caesar, and give to GOD, what belongs to GOD." Mark 12:14-17.
P: "Does the law permit a person to work by healing on the Sabbath?"
J: "If you had a sheep that fell into a well on the Sabbath, wouldn't you work to pull it out? Of course, you would." Matthew 5:10-11.
P: "This woman was caught in the act of adultery. The law of Moses says to stone her. What do you say?"

J: "All right, but let the one who has never sinned throw the first stone." John 8:4-7.
P: Silence there were no further questions. The judgment is for Jesus and mankind! Case closed.

JESUS, testifying FOR THE FATHER:
1) The most important commandment in the law of Moses, Jesus said, is "You must love the Lord our GOD with all your heart, all your soul, and all your mind." Matthew 22:36-37.
2) When missing for three days, the searching Mary and Joseph found Jesus in the Temple. Jesus asked "But why did you need to search? Didn't you know that I must be in my Father's house about my Father's business?" Luke 2:49.
3) "My nourishment comes from doing the will of GOD who sent me, and from finishing His work." John 4:34.
4) Just before His arrest, Jesus prayed. "Father, if you are willing, please take this cup of suffering away from me. Yet I want your will to be done, not mine." Luke 22:42.

Jesus proves His case: Our Beloved Savior and GOD's Beloved Son.

Something to think about.

67. MEDIATOR

A mediator is one who acts as an intermediary to work
with opposing sides in order to bring about a settlement-
-an attempt to influence a disagreement between two or
more parties with the goal of resolving the dispute,
especially if the case is going to court.

For several years after retiring from the bench as a circuit
court judge, I opened my own mediation business based
in Rapid City, South Dakota. During that time, I
mediated hundreds of cases, helping people resolve their
differences and settle pending lawsuits. The experience
as a trial judge was of great benefit since I understood the
legal issues involved, could relate to the attorneys, and tell
the parties from first-hand knowledge and experience the
time, effort, worry, stress, and uncertainty, involved in a
protracted lawsuit and possible jury trial.

My mediation work involved disagreements between man.
What about the differences between GOD's law and man's
sinful nature?

The dispute: GOD hates sin; yet, man sins! "There is no
one righteous, not even one." Romans 3:10. "Everyone
who sins is breaking GOD's law, for all sin is contrary to
the law of GOD." 1 John 3:4. "The wages of sin is death."
Romans 6:23. Without a mediator we are destined for an
eternity in hell. And who knows both the Father and the
struggles of mankind?

"There is one God and one Mediator who can reconcile God and humanity -- the man Jesus Christ." 1 Timothy 2:5. "For God made Christ, who never sinned, to be the offering for our sin, so that we could be made right with God through Christ." 2 Corinthians 5:21. Jesus is the sacrifice that atones for our sins.

"There is salvation in no one else! God has given no other name under heaven by which we must be saved." Acts 4:12. Jesus is your Savior, your mediator, and your assurance of salvation.

Something to think about.

so that your faith might not rest in the wisdom of men but in the power of God.
1 Corinthians 2:5

Graphic from the YouVersion Bible app

68. SPIRITUAL WISDOM.

Wisdom is defined as a combination of experience, knowledge, and good judgment. Most comes through experience and application. You are wiser as a result of failures, successes, and the school of "hard knocks". You can increase wisdom by soaking up the wisdom of others.

Paul delivered a message of wisdom in 1 Corinthians Chapter 4. He said when he came to visit, he did not use lofty words and impressive wisdom to deliver GOD's secret plan. He only passed on what Jesus said. "Rather than using clever and persuasive speeches, I relied only on the power of the Holy Spirit. I did this so you would trust not in human wisdom but in the power of GOD." 1 Corinthians 2:4-5.

Usable wisdom comes from GOD the Father.

Something to think about.

69. KNOWING GOD'S WILL FOR YOU.

The Bible is truly the gift that never stops giving, to wit: Paul stated the following: "Don't copy the behavior and customs of this world, but let GOD transform you into a new person by changing the way you think. <u>Then you will learn to know GOD's will for you</u>, which is good and pleasing and <u>perfect</u>." Romans 12:2.

<u>GOD's PLAN</u>: "Even before He made the world, GOD loved us and chose us in Christ to be holy and without fault in His eyes. GOD decided in advance to adopt us into His own family by bringing us to Himself through Jesus Christ." Ephesians 1:4-5. GOD's "will" for you at creation is salvation --- entering His Kingdom forever.

<u>GOD's SPIRITUAL GIFTS</u>: "In his grace, GOD has given us different gifts for doing different things well. So if GOD has given you the ability to prophesy, speak out with as much faith as GOD has given you. If your gift is serving others, serve them well. If you are a teacher, teach well. If your gift is encouraging others, be encouraging. If it is giving, give generously. If GOD has given you leadership ability, take the responsibility seriously. And if you have a gift for showing kindness to others, do it gladly." Romans 12:6-8. GOD's will for you while here is to SERVE others.

<u>God's SON</u>: "I am the way, the truth, and the life. No one can come to the Father except through me." John 14:6. Very plain, very understandable! And when the world offers only a craving for physical pleasure, a craving for everything we see, and pride in our achievements and possessions (1 John 2:35-16), we have the love and assurance of Jesus: "But take heart, because I have overcome the world". John 16:33. God's will is for you to live and love like Jesus.

"Then a voice from the cloud said, 'This is my Son, my Chosen One. <u>Listen to him.</u>'" Luke 9:35.

<u>God's WILL</u> for you is salvation with Him; you performing your spiritual gift for your fellow-man; you transforming your thinking to overcome the world and your sinful nature; all of which can only be accomplished through His Son, Jesus Christ, "the way, the truth, and the life."

Something to think about.

70. BOOMERANG

A boomerang is a throwing tool. It is one of the oldest innovations, and often associated with the aboriginal people of Australia. The unique feature is, when thrown properly, the tool returns back to you. The Bible had this tool long before the boomerang was popular.

"I will never fail you. I will never abandon you." Hebrews 13:5. "No power in the sky above or in the earth below -- indeed, nothing in all creation will ever be able to separate us from the love of God that is revealed in Christ Jesus our Lord." Romans 8:39. "Christ suffered for our sins once for all time." 1 Peter 3:18.

God has given all of this to us through His kindness and grace, and yet we can find ourselves ignoring, rejecting and---dare I say, "throwing" God away. It is unfathomable that God would treat our unappreciation and sinfulness with undeserved patience, forgiveness, and return -- yet that is our God! Despite our voluntary separation, "He does not want anyone to be destroyed, but wants everyone to repent." 2 Peter 3:9.

God is our spiritual boomerang! No matter how far or how often we "throw" Him, when we repent, He returns to us. Repent. And when God returns to you, do not again make the mistake thinking you can live without Him.

"Those who have been born into GOD's family do not make a practice of sinning, because GOD's life is in them. So they can't keep sinning, <u>because they are children of GOD.</u>" 1 JOHN 3:9.

Something to think about.

P.S. And don't forget the "return" of Jesus will come unexpectedly like a thief in the night (see 1 Thessalonians 5:2)

71. Our Father Who Art In Heaven.....

"When you pray, don't babble on and on as people of other religions do. They think their prayers are answered merely by repeating their words again and again. Don't be like them for your Father knows exactly what you need even before you ask him! Pray like this:" Matthew 6:7-13. Let's take some time to examine the implications and commitment stated in the prayer to our Father in heaven.

"Our Father who art in heaven, hallowed be your name." This acknowledges the existence of God; He created the world and us; heaven exists; His name is treated as exalted, sacred, and holy, most deserving of all our praise and love.

"Thy Kingdom come, thy will be done on earth as it is in heaven." This acknowledges that God has a final eternal resting place for "His children"; acknowledges we should think God's ways and thoughts, behave in accordance with God's standards to assure His will be done here on this earth, as we know it is in heaven. (If we can do God's will on earth Satan will be "Out of Business")!

"Give us this day our daily bread." We don't worry about our earthly needs. "Seek the Kingdom of God above all else, and live righteously, and he will give you everything you need." Matthew 6:33. "I am the bread of life" John 6:35.

"Forgive us our trespasses, as we forgive those who trespass against us." If you don't forgive others, GOD does not forgive you! Abide by this request/promise to GOD, and discrimination, hatred, hurt, persecution, and disrespect no longer exist.

"Lead us not into temptation, but deliver us from evil." We ask help to not yield to earthly desires, and protection from the evil one (Satan), the enemy of God.

"For thine is the Kingdom, the power, and the glory forever and ever." A final acknowledgement that GOD is in control, His Kingdom awaits us with eternal life.

"GOD himself will be with them. He will wipe every tear from their eyes, and there will be no more death or sorrow or crying or pain. All of these things will be gone forever." Revelations 21:3-4.

Something to "pray" about.

72. THE LITTLE RED HEN.

The Little Red Hen is a children's fable wherein the Red
Hen has a wheat seed to plant and asks some animals (cat,
duck, & pig) from the barnyard to assist her. They all
decline. The story proceeds through the various stages of
planting, harvesting, threshing, milling, and baking into
bread, all of which the Red Hen asks for assistance. All
the animals continue to decline giving assistance. After
baking, the Red Hen asked who would help eat the bread.
The animals all agreed to help eat the bread. The Red
Hen declined stating she had done all the work so she
(and her chicks) would eat the bread. Applying the Bible
(God's Word) makes this story most profound.

SEED: God creates us as *individual* seeds for planting.
(see Isaiah 44:24, your redeemer, who formed you from
the womb).

WORK ETHIC: Paul told the Thessalonians: "Those
unwilling to work will not get to eat"; such people are
commanded and urged in the name of the Lord Jesus
Christ to settle down and work to earn their own living
(see 2 Thessalonians 3:10-12). Let's be clear, Paul is
talking about the *unwilling* not the *unable*! You have an
obligation to support the unable and an obligation NOT
to support the freeloader. Resources which could help
the helpless are wasted when given to the lazy, and serves
only to enable them.

INDIVIDUAL PLANTING: Knowing God's expectation for us to grow for his glory, we hear God's word, accept God's word, and we "plant" ourselves in good soil so we can produce a bountiful harvest (feed many from one seed). We do not allow Satan, the trials/tribulations of this world, or the deceit, desires, and riches of this world to destroy our seed (see Mark 4:3-20, Parable of the Sower).

ASSIGNED PLANTING: We, in turn, plant seed by taking God's word to others. We are obligated to tell others the Good News about the wonderful grace of God. (see Acts 20:24). We "rescue others by snatching them from the flames of judgment." Jude 23.

BREAD/SALVATION: The Red Hen and chicks enjoyed the bread. God and His "chicks" (Children of God) enjoy salvation FOREVER!

Something to think about.

Photo by James Chan

73. NO WAY -- ABSOLUTELY NO WAY!

The above phrase is used to emphasize that you <u>REALLY</u> mean no. It's not going to happen! Undoubtedly your response if you are requested to ride a Brama Bull in a rodeo or walk a tightrope over the Grand Canyon!

Do you have the same "No Way" for your soul?

- No Way am I going to relinquish the salvation earned for me through the crucifixion and resurrection of Jesus Christ ---- No Way!
- No Way am I going to let anyone or anything interfere negatively with my relationship with GOD --- No Way!
- No Way am I going to purposely disappoint GOD --- No Way!
- No Way am I going to forget GOD's plan for me (His Kingdom) --- No Way!
- No way am I going to ignore that this life has trials and tribulations --- No Way!
- No Way am I going to spend my eternal life <u>with the devil</u> --- *Absolutely*. No. Way!

Something to "No Way" about!

SOME OF GOD'S POSITIVES.

Throughout this book of devotions are matters to reflect upon and, at times, some blunt realities of GOD's expected behavior. This notwithstanding, please remember you cannot do anything to escape GOD's love. We can get discouraged and feel unworthy of GOD's love, but we should be strengthened by knowing GOD's grace is a gift, and available in abundance. So, we need not feel inferior or undeserving. Don't look at your perceived negatives, rather remind yourself of GOD's positives, a few of which are noted below.

Review these often and feel GOD's love, the desire for a relationship, and knowledge that *GOD will never abandon you*!

1. Before GOD made the world, He had a plan of salvation for each of us. Jeremiah (see 1:5 & 29:11 and Ephesians 1:4-5).
2. You cannot separate yourself from GOD's UNCONDITIONAL love (see Romans 8:31-39).
3. GOD so loved the world He gave his only son so you would not perish, but have eternal life (see John 3:16).
4. Jesus died for your sins (see 1 Peter 3:18).
5. Jesus was raised from the dead and lives still (see Matthew 28:5-10).
6. Jesus is the only way to salvation (the way, the truth, and the life (see John 14:6).

7. Jesus, through His death and resurrection, destroyed death and our fear of death (see Hebrews 2:14-15).
8. Perfect Love: such love has no fear, because PERFECT LOVE EXPELS ALL FEARS. (see 1 John 4:16-18). (We have neither fear of living nor fear of dying -- we can face him with confidence because we live like Jesus here in this world).
9. If God is for us who can be against us? (see Romans 8:31).
   - His understanding is unfathomable (see Isaiah 40:28).
   - His decisions and ways are unfathomable (see Romans 11:33).
   - His love is unfathomable (see Ephesians 3:18-19).
   - His Kingdom is unfathomable (see 2 Corinthians 9).
10. God forgives and forgets, no matter how great the sin (see Hebrews 8:12).
11. Forget the past – focus on salvation that lies ahead (see Philippians 3:13-14).
12. God will never fail you; never abandon you; the Lord is your helper, so you will have no fear (see Hebrews 13:5-6).
13. God will not test you beyond your strength and shows you a way out (see 1 Corinthians 10:13).

14. GOD assures Salvation for "believers" (see Romans 10:9-13).
15. GOD shows no favoritism. We are all equal in His eyes (see Romans 2:11).
16. GOD told us about heaven, (see 1 Corinthians 2:9); and hell with the devil, (see Revelation 20:12). Warns us about the devil (see 1 Peter 5:8-9).
17. Jesus says always be joyful. Never stop praying. Be thankful in all circumstances (see 1 Thessalonians 16-18). We can do this because of the promise of salvation (see 1 Peter 1:3-9).
18. GOD created the world; created us; gave us Moses and the 10 commandments; the prophets; His only son, Jesus, to die for our sins, rise from the dead, and gain eternal life through faith in Jesus; the teachings of Jesus; the Holy Spirit; the apostles; the four gospels, Paul and other writers; the old and new testament; and daily reminders to pray and be strong so we can enjoy a satisfying, joy-filled everlasting life.
19. "Here on earth you will have many trials and sorrows. But take heart, *I have overcome the world.*" Jesus in John 16:33.

GO WITH THE POSITIVES AND FEEL CONFIDENCE IN YOUR FAITH!

Plenty to Think About!

"Watch out that you do not lose what we have worked so hard to achieve. Be diligent so that you receive your full reward." 2 John 8.

About the Author

Eugene L. Martin is not, except maybe in his family's eyes, a best-selling author. He did, however, earn his law degree from the University of South Dakota Law School just before being drafted to serve in the United States Army during the Vietnam War (1968-1970). Afterward, he practiced law in his hometown, including a stint as City Attorney. He was appointed Circuit Court Trial Judge for the State of South Dakota serving in that capacity for 23 years. A circuit judge presides over such criminal actions as assaults, murder, manslaughter, theft, burglary, rape, driving while intoxicated, plus civil actions like negligence and personal injuries, breach of contract, divorces, custody battles, visitation rights, adoptions (his favorite), juvenile matters including delinquency, children in need of supervision, and abused or neglected children, and more. When Martin retired from the bench, he provided legal settlement services via mediation and arbitration. He is now fully retired and resides in Rapid City, South Dakota with his wife, Sandra. They are blessed with three amazing children, two tremendous sons-in-law, and two of the best granddaughters in the world!

"Not that I have already .... been made perfect, but I press on to take hold of that for which Christ Jesus took hold of me...But one thing I do: forgetting what is behind and straining toward what is ahead, I press on toward the goal to win the prize for which God has called me heavenward in Christ Jesus." Philippians 3:12-14 NIV.